C000041802

Azure Data Lake
Complete Self-Assessment Guide

The guidance in this Self-Assessment is based on Azure Data Lake best practices and standards in business process architecture, design and quality management. The guidance is also based on the professional judgment of the individual collaborators listed in the Acknowledgments.

Notice of rights

You are licensed to use the Self-Assessment contents in your presentations and materials for internal use and customers without asking us - we are here to help.

All rights reserved for the book itself: this book may not be reproduced or transmitted in any form by any means, electronic, mechanical, photocopying, recording, or otherwise, without the prior written permission of the publisher.

The information in this book is distributed on an "As Is" basis without warranty. While every precaution has been taken in the preparation of he book, neither the author nor the publisher shall have any liability to any person or entity with respect to any loss or damage caused or alleged to be caused directly or indirectly by the instructions contained in this book or by the products described in it.

Trademarks

Many of the designations used by manufacturers and sellers to distinguish their products are claimed as trademarks. Where those designations appear in this book, and the publisher was aware of a trademark claim, the designations appear as requested by the owner of the trademark. All other product names and services identified throughout this book are used in editorial fashion only and for the benefit of such companies with no intention of infringement of the trademark. No such use, or the use of any trade name, is intended to convey endorsement or other affiliation with this book.

Copyright © by The Art of Service
http://theartofservice.com
service@theartofservice.com

Table of Contents

About The Art of Service

The Art of Service, Business Process Architects since 2000, is dedicated to helping stakeholders achieve excellence.

Defining, designing, creating, and implementing a process to solve a stakeholders challenge or meet an objective is the most valuable role… In EVERY group, company, organization and department.

Unless you're talking a one-time, single-use project, there should be a process. Whether that process is managed and implemented by humans, AI, or a combination of the two, it needs to be designed by someone with a complex enough perspective to ask the right questions.

Someone capable of asking the right questions and step back and say, 'What are we really trying to accomplish here? And is there a different way to look at it?'

With The Art of Service's Standard Requirements Self-Assessments, we empower people who can do just that — whether their title is marketer, entrepreneur, manager, salesperson, consultant, Business Process Manager, executive assistant, IT Manager, CIO etc... —they are the people who rule the future. They are people who watch the process as it happens, and ask the right questions to make the process work better.

Contact us when you need any support with this Self-Assessment and any help with templates, blue-prints and examples of standard documents you might need:

http://theartofservice.com
service@theartofservice.com

Acknowledgments

This checklist was developed under the auspices of The Art of Service, chaired by Gerardus Blokdyk.

Representatives from several client companies participated in the preparation of this Self-Assessment.

In addition, we are thankful for the design and printing services provided.

Included Resources - how to access

Included with your purchase of the book is the Azure Data Lake Self-Assessment Spreadsheet Dashboard which contains all questions and Self-Assessment areas and auto-generates insights, graphs, and project RACI planning - all with examples to get you started right away.

How? Simply send an email to
access@theartofservice.com
with this books' title in the subject to get the Azure Data Lake Self Assessment Tool right away.

You will receive the following contents with New and Updated specific criteria:

- The latest quick edition of the book in PDF

- The latest complete edition of the book in PDF, which criteria correspond to the criteria in...

- The Self-Assessment Excel Dashboard, and...

- Example pre-filled Self-Assessment Excel Dashboard to get familiar with results generation

- In-depth specific Checklists covering the topic

- Project management checklists and templates to assist with implementation

INCLUDES LIFETIME SELF ASSESSMENT UPDATES

Every self assessment comes with Lifetime Updates and Lifetime Free Updated Books. Lifetime Updates is an industry-first feature which allows you to receive verified self assessment updates, ensuring you always have the most accurate information at your fingertips.

Get it now- you will be glad you did - do it now, before you forget.

Send an email to **access@theartofservice.com** with this books' title in the subject to get the Azure Data Lake Self Assessment Tool right away.

Your feedback is invaluable to us

If you recently bought this book, we would love to hear from you! You can do this by writing a review on amazon (or the online store where you purchased this book) about your last purchase! As part of our continual service improvement process, we love to hear real client experiences and feedback.

How does it work?
To post a review on Amazon, just log in to your account and click on the Create Your Own Review button (under Customer Reviews) of the relevant product page. You can find examples of product reviews in Amazon. If you purchased from another online store, simply follow their procedures.

What happens when I submit my review?
Once you have submitted your review, send us an email at review@theartofservice.com with the link to your review so we can properly thank you for your feedback.

Purpose of this Self-Assessment

This Self-Assessment has been developed to improve understanding of the requirements and elements of Azure Data Lake, based on best practices and standards in business process architecture, design and quality management.

It is designed to allow for a rapid Self-Assessment to determine how closely existing management practices and procedures correspond to the elements of the Self-Assessment.

The criteria of requirements and elements of Azure Data Lake have been rephrased in the format of a Self-Assessment questionnaire, with a seven-criterion scoring system, as explained in this document.

In this format, even with limited background knowledge of Azure

Data Lake, a manager can quickly review existing operations to determine how they measure up to the standards. This in turn can serve as the starting point of a 'gap analysis' to identify management tools or system elements that might usefully be implemented in the organization to help improve overall performance.

How to use the Self-Assessment

On the following pages are a series of questions to identify to what extent your Azure Data Lake initiative is complete in comparison to the requirements set in standards.

To facilitate answering the questions, there is a space in front of each question to enter a score on a scale of '1' to '5'.

1 Strongly Disagree

2 Disagree

3 Neutral

4 Agree

5 Strongly Agree

Read the question and rate it with the following in front of mind:

'In my belief, the answer to this question is clearly defined'.

There are two ways in which you can choose to interpret this statement;
1. how aware are you that the answer to the question is clearly defined
2. for more in-depth analysis you can choose to gather

evidence and confirm the answer to the question. This obviously will take more time, most Self-Assessment users opt for the first way to interpret the question and dig deeper later on based on the outcome of the overall Self-Assessment.

A score of '1' would mean that the answer is not clear at all, where a '5' would mean the answer is crystal clear and defined. Leave emtpy when the question is not applicable or you don't want to answer it, you can skip it without affecting your score. Write your score in the space provided.

After you have responded to all the appropriate statements in each section, compute your average score for that section, using the formula provided, and round to the nearest tenth. Then transfer to the corresponding spoke in the Azure Data Lake Scorecard on the second next page of the Self-Assessment.

Your completed Azure Data Lake Scorecard will give you a clear presentation of which Azure Data Lake areas need attention.

Azure Data Lake
Scorecard Example

Example of how the finalized Scorecard can look like:

Azure Data Lake Scorecard

Your Scores:

BEGINNING OF THE SELF-ASSESSMENT:

CRITERION #1: RECOGNIZE

INTENT: Be aware of the need for change. Recognize that there is an unfavorable variation, problem or symptom.

In my belief, the answer to this question is clearly defined:

5 Strongly Agree

4 Agree

3 Neutral

2 Disagree

1 Strongly Disagree

1. What do you need to start doing?
<--- Score

2. Do you know what you need to know about Azure Data Lake?
<--- Score

3. Will a response program recognize when a crisis occurs and provide some level of response?

<--- Score

4. Have you identified your Azure Data Lake key performance indicators?
<--- Score

5. What are the expected benefits of Azure Data Lake to the business?
<--- Score

6. Will new equipment/products be required to facilitate Azure Data Lake delivery, for example is new software needed?
<--- Score

7. Are your goals realistic? Do you need to redefine your problem? Perhaps the problem has changed or maybe you have reached your goal and need to set a new one?
<--- Score

8. What is the problem or issue?
<--- Score

9. To what extent would your organization benefit from being recognized as a award recipient?
<--- Score

10. Who needs what information?
<--- Score

11. Who defines the rules in relation to any given issue?
<--- Score

12. How are you going to measure success?

<--- Score

13. What needs to be done?
<--- Score

14. What should be considered when identifying available resources, constraints, and deadlines?
<--- Score

15. Does Azure Data Lake create potential expectations in other areas that need to be recognized and considered?
<--- Score

16. How does it fit into your organizational needs and tasks?
<--- Score

17. What is the smallest subset of the problem you can usefully solve?
<--- Score

18. Think about the people you identified for your Azure Data Lake project and the project responsibilities you would assign to them. what kind of training do you think they would need to perform these responsibilities effectively?
<--- Score

19. Are there any specific expectations or concerns about the Azure Data Lake team, Azure Data Lake itself?
<--- Score

20. What situation(s) led to this Azure Data Lake Self Assessment?

<--- Score

21. To what extent does each concerned units management team recognize Azure Data Lake as an effective investment?
<--- Score

22. Can management personnel recognize the monetary benefit of Azure Data Lake?
<--- Score

23. What are the minority interests and what amount of minority interests can be recognized?
<--- Score

24. As a sponsor, customer or management, how important is it to meet goals, objectives?
<--- Score

25. Do you need to avoid or amend any Azure Data Lake activities?
<--- Score

26. How much are sponsors, customers, partners, stakeholders involved in Azure Data Lake? In other words, what are the risks, if Azure Data Lake does not deliver successfully?
<--- Score

27. What is the clients problem or need?
<--- Score

28. What are the business objectives to be achieved with Azure Data Lake?
<--- Score

29. What tools and technologies are needed for a custom Azure Data Lake project?
<--- Score

30. What kind of support is needed?
<--- Score

31. What is the business problem?
<--- Score

32. Does your organization need more Azure Data Lake education?
<--- Score

33. Will Azure Data Lake deliverables need to be tested and, if so, by whom?
<--- Score

34. Consider your own Azure Data Lake project, what types of organizational problems do you think might be causing or affecting your problem, based on the work done so far?
<--- Score

35. Are problem definition and motivation clearly presented?
<--- Score

36. What information do users need?
<--- Score

37. Are there Azure Data Lake problems defined?
<--- Score

38. How are the Azure Data Lake's objectives aligned to the organization's overall business strategy?

<--- Score

39. Looking at each person individually – does every one have the qualities which are needed to work in this group?
<--- Score

40. Does aggregation exceed permissible need to know about an individual?
<--- Score

41. Who had the original idea?
<--- Score

42. Are there recognized Azure Data Lake problems?
<--- Score

43. Do you need all the infrastructure up all of the time to manage throughout your build?
<--- Score

44. For your Azure Data Lake project, identify and describe the business environment, is there more than one layer to the business environment?
<--- Score

45. You need to gather information that you can use to debug the job. Which tool do you use?
<--- Score

46. Are controls defined to recognize and contain problems?
<--- Score

47. When a Azure Data Lake manager recognizes a problem, what options are available?

<--- Score

48. What else needs to be measured?
<--- Score

49. Who are your key stakeholders who need to sign off?
<--- Score

50. What are your needs in relation to Azure Data Lake skills, labor, equipment, and markets?
<--- Score

51. Is the need for organizational change recognized?
<--- Score

52. Are you dealing with any of the same issues today as yesterday? What can you do about this?
<--- Score

53. What are the timeframes required to resolve each of the issues/problems?
<--- Score

54. Will it solve real problems?
<--- Score

55. Who needs to know about Azure Data Lake?
<--- Score

56. How do you take a forward-looking perspective in identifying Azure Data Lake research related to market response and models?
<--- Score

57. What makes this problem worth solving?

<--- Score

58. Should you invest in industry-recognized qualications?
<--- Score

59. Is it clear when you think of the day ahead of you what activities and tasks you need to complete?
<--- Score

60. What do you need to do to get there?
<--- Score

61. Do you need different information or graphics?
<--- Score

62. How can auditing be a preventative security measure?
<--- Score

63. What additional tools do you need?
<--- Score

64. Do you have/need 24-hour access to key personnel?
<--- Score

65. How do you assess your Azure Data Lake workforce capability and capacity needs, including skills, competencies, and staffing levels?
<--- Score

66. How do you identify the kinds of information that you will need?
<--- Score

67. What activities does the governance board need to consider?
<--- Score

68. What extra resources will you need?
<--- Score

69. Are there any revenue recognition issues?
<--- Score

70. Who else hopes to benefit from it?
<--- Score

71. What prevents you from making the changes you know will make you a more effective Azure Data Lake leader?
<--- Score

72. What training and capacity building actions are needed to implement proposed reforms?
<--- Score

73. What problems are you facing and how do you consider Azure Data Lake will circumvent those obstacles?
<--- Score

74. Are employees recognized or rewarded for performance that demonstrates the highest levels of integrity?
<--- Score

75. What vendors make products that address the Azure Data Lake needs?
<--- Score

76. What does Azure Data Lake success mean to the stakeholders?
<--- Score

77. What would happen if Azure Data Lake weren't done?
<--- Score

Add up total points for this section:
_ _ _ _ _ = Total points for this section

Divided by: _ _ _ _ _ _ (number of statements answered) = _ _ _ _ _ _
Average score for this section

Transfer your score to the Azure Data Lake Index at the beginning of the Self-Assessment.

CRITERION #2: DEFINE:

INTENT: Formulate the business problem. Define the problem, needs and objectives.

In my belief, the answer to this question is clearly defined:

5 Strongly Agree

4 Agree

3 Neutral

2 Disagree

1 Strongly Disagree

1. What happens if Azure Data Lake's scope changes?
<--- Score

2. Is the team adequately staffed with the desired cross-functionality? If not, what additional resources are available to the team?
<--- Score

3. Is there a completed, verified, and validated high-

level 'as is' (not 'should be' or 'could be') business process map?
<--- Score

4. Is the Azure Data Lake scope manageable?
<--- Score

5. Is Azure Data Lake linked to key business goals and objectives?
<--- Score

6. Is the improvement team aware of the different versions of a process: what they think it is vs. what it actually is vs. what it should be vs. what it could be?
<--- Score

7. Will team members perform Azure Data Lake work when assigned and in a timely fashion?
<--- Score

8. Who defines (or who defined) the rules and roles?
<--- Score

9. Are customer(s) identified and segmented according to their different needs and requirements?
<--- Score

10. How would you define the culture at your organization, how susceptible is it to Azure Data Lake changes?
<--- Score

11. Does the team have regular meetings?
<--- Score

12. Is there a critical path to deliver Azure Data Lake

results?
<--- Score

13. What key business process output measure(s) does Azure Data Lake leverage and how?
<--- Score

14. What are the boundaries of the scope? What is in bounds and what is not? What is the start point? What is the stop point?
<--- Score

15. Are business processes mapped?
<--- Score

16. How do you keep key subject matter experts in the loop?
<--- Score

17. Is there a Azure Data Lake management charter, including business case, problem and goal statements, scope, milestones, roles and responsibilities, communication plan?
<--- Score

18. What is in scope?
<--- Score

19. How was the 'as is' process map developed, reviewed, verified and validated?
<--- Score

20. Will team members regularly document their Azure Data Lake work?
<--- Score

21. Are roles and responsibilities formally defined?
<--- Score

22. What are the Roles and Responsibilities for each team member and its leadership? Where is this documented?
<--- Score

23. How do you gather Azure Data Lake requirements?
<--- Score

24. What would be the goal or target for a Azure Data Lake's improvement team?
<--- Score

25. What is the definition of success?
<--- Score

26. How will the Azure Data Lake team and the organization measure complete success of Azure Data Lake?
<--- Score

27. What are the dynamics of the communication plan?
<--- Score

28. Is there a completed SIPOC representation, describing the Suppliers, Inputs, Process, Outputs, and Customers?
<--- Score

29. Are team charters developed?
<--- Score

30. What are the compelling business reasons for embarking on Azure Data Lake?
<--- Score

31. Who are the Azure Data Lake improvement team members, including Management Leads and Coaches?
<--- Score

32. Does the scope remain the same?
<--- Score

33. What is in Scope?
<--- Score

34. Are improvement team members fully trained on Azure Data Lake?
<--- Score

35. Do the problem and goal statements meet the SMART criteria (specific, measurable, attainable, relevant, and time-bound)?
<--- Score

36. What are the record-keeping requirements of Azure Data Lake activities?
<--- Score

37. What is out-of-scope initially?
<--- Score

38. What is the scope?
<--- Score

39. Is the team formed and are team leaders (Coaches and Management Leads) assigned?

<--- Score

40. Are approval levels defined for contracts and supplements to contracts?
<--- Score

41. Has the Azure Data Lake work been fairly and/or equitably divided and delegated among team members who are qualified and capable to perform the work? Has everyone contributed?
<--- Score

42. When are meeting minutes sent out? Who is on the distribution list?
<--- Score

43. Is the team equipped with available and reliable resources?
<--- Score

44. Is the scope of Azure Data Lake defined?
<--- Score

45. Has anyone else (internal or external to the organization) attempted to solve this problem or a similar one before? If so, what knowledge can be leveraged from these previous efforts?
<--- Score

46. Who is gathering Azure Data Lake information?
<--- Score

47. Is data collected and displayed to better understand customer(s) critical needs and requirements.
<--- Score

48. What constraints exist that might impact the team?

<--- Score

49. Are different versions of process maps needed to account for the different types of inputs?

<--- Score

50. Is scope creep really all bad news?

<--- Score

51. Has/have the customer(s) been identified?

<--- Score

52. How did the Azure Data Lake manager receive input to the development of a Azure Data Lake improvement plan and the estimated completion dates/times of each activity?

<--- Score

53. Are resources adequate for the scope?

<--- Score

54. In what way can you redefine the criteria of choice clients have in your category in your favor?

<--- Score

55. What would you propose as a good business case for virtualizing the desktop (offering VDI)?

<--- Score

56. Are there any constraints known that bear on the ability to perform Azure Data Lake work? How is the team addressing them?

<--- Score

57. Scope of sensitive information?
<--- Score

58. How does the Azure Data Lake manager ensure against scope creep?
<--- Score

59. Is Azure Data Lake required?
<--- Score

60. What specifically is the problem? Where does it occur? When does it occur? What is its extent?
<--- Score

61. How is the team tracking and documenting its work?
<--- Score

62. If substitutes have been appointed, have they been briefed on the Azure Data Lake goals and received regular communications as to the progress to date?
<--- Score

63. What Azure Data Lake requirements should be gathered?
<--- Score

64. Have specific policy objectives been defined?
<--- Score

65. Have all basic functions of Azure Data Lake been defined?
<--- Score

66. How often are the team meetings?
<--- Score

67. What system do you use for gathering Azure Data Lake information?
<--- Score

68. How can the value of Azure Data Lake be defined?
<--- Score

69. What is out of scope?
<--- Score

70. How do you hand over Azure Data Lake context?
<--- Score

71. What sources do you use to gather information for a Azure Data Lake study?
<--- Score

72. Is full participation by members in regularly held team meetings guaranteed?
<--- Score

73. Has a project plan, Gantt chart, or similar been developed/completed?
<--- Score

74. Are required metrics defined, what are they?
<--- Score

75. Is the team sponsored by a champion or business leader?
<--- Score

76. Has the direction changed at all during the course

of Azure Data Lake? If so, when did it change and why?

<--- Score

77. What is the context?

<--- Score

78. How to model context in a computational environment?

<--- Score

79. Is the current 'as is' process being followed? If not, what are the discrepancies?

<--- Score

80. Is there regularly 100% attendance at the team meetings? If not, have appointed substitutes attended to preserve cross-functionality and full representation?

<--- Score

81. How will variation in the actual durations of each activity be dealt with to ensure that the expected Azure Data Lake results are met?

<--- Score

82. What scope to assess?

<--- Score

83. Why are you doing Azure Data Lake and what is the scope?

<--- Score

84. Is it clearly defined in and to your organization what you do?

<--- Score

85. Is the Azure Data Lake scope complete and appropriately sized?
<--- Score

86. What customer feedback methods were used to solicit their input?
<--- Score

87. What are the rough order estimates on cost savings/opportunities that Azure Data Lake brings?
<--- Score

88. What scope do you want your strategy to cover?
<--- Score

89. Are audit criteria, scope, frequency and methods defined?
<--- Score

90. What is the scope of the Azure Data Lake effort?
<--- Score

91. What are the tasks and definitions?
<--- Score

92. How and when will the baselines be defined?
<--- Score

93. What is the scope of Azure Data Lake?
<--- Score

94. Are accountability and ownership for Azure Data Lake clearly defined?
<--- Score

95. When is the estimated completion date?
<--- Score

96. How do you manage scope?
<--- Score

97. Have all of the relationships been defined properly?
<--- Score

98. Are task requirements clearly defined?
<--- Score

99. Has your scope been defined?
<--- Score

100. Has a team charter been developed and communicated?
<--- Score

101. Have the customer needs been translated into specific, measurable requirements? How?
<--- Score

102. How do you think the partners involved in Azure Data Lake would have defined success?
<--- Score

103. What is in the scope and what is not in scope?
<--- Score

104. Is Azure Data Lake currently on schedule according to the plan?
<--- Score

105. Has everyone on the team, including the team

leaders, been properly trained?
<--- Score

106. What critical content must be communicated –
who, what, when, where, and how?
<--- Score

107. Has a high-level 'as is' process map been
completed, verified and validated?
<--- Score

108. What was the context?
<--- Score

109. What baselines are required to be defined and
managed?
<--- Score

110. Has the improvement team collected the 'voice
of the customer' (obtained feedback – qualitative and
quantitative)?
<--- Score

111. What defines best in class?
<--- Score

112. Are customers identified and high impact areas
defined?
<--- Score

113. Is a fully trained team formed, supported,
and committed to work on the Azure Data Lake
improvements?
<--- Score

114. When was the Azure Data Lake start date?

<--- Score

115. Do you all define Azure Data Lake in the same way?
<--- Score

116. Are there different segments of customers?
<--- Score

Add up total points for this section:
_ _ _ _ _ = Total points for this section

Divided by: _ _ _ _ _ _ (number of statements answered) = _ _ _ _ _ _
Average score for this section

Transfer your score to the Azure Data Lake Index at the beginning of the Self-Assessment.

CRITERION #3: MEASURE:

INTENT: Gather the correct data.
Measure the current performance and
evolution of the situation.

In my belief, the answer to this
question is clearly defined:

5 Strongly Agree

4 Agree

3 Neutral

2 Disagree

1 Strongly Disagree

1. How will the success of the project be measured, and what are the criteria for continued funding?
<--- Score

2. Why do you expend time and effort to implement measurement, for whom?
<--- Score

3. Does Azure Data Lake analysis isolate the

fundamental causes of problems?

<--- Score

4. While a move from Oracle's MySQL may be necessary because of its inability to handle key big data use cases, why should that move involve a switch to Apache Cassandra and DataStax Enterprise?

<--- Score

5. Can we measure the basic performance measures consistently and comprehensively?

<--- Score

6. Does the Azure Data Lake task fit the client's priorities?

<--- Score

7. What charts has the team used to display the components of variation in the process?

<--- Score

8. What key measures identified indicate the performance of the business process?

<--- Score

9. What are some impacts of Big Data?

<--- Score

10. Have the types of risks that may impact Azure Data Lake been identified and analyzed?

<--- Score

11. What are the uncertainties surrounding estimates of impact?

<--- Score

12. What evidence is there and what is measured?
<--- Score

13. How do we measure the efficiency of these algorithms?
<--- Score

14. Business impact/achieved results - what short-term and long-term benefits were achieved through this solution?
<--- Score

15. What could cause delays in the schedule?
<--- Score

16. Why analysis inside a DBMS?
<--- Score

17. What new analytical possibilities would open up for our organization if you aggregated all available data into a central data lake for in-depth and ongoing analysis?
<--- Score

18. Can analyses improve with more data to process?
<--- Score

19. How are the current generation of managers and auditors placed to interpret the result of Big Data analysis?
<--- Score

20. Are missed Azure Data Lake opportunities costing your organization money?

<--- Score

21. Are key measures identified and agreed upon?
<--- Score

22. What causes investor action?
<--- Score

23. Is data collected on key measures that were identified?
<--- Score

24. With more data to analyze, can Big Data improve decision-making?
<--- Score

25. What are your key Azure Data Lake indicators that you will measure, analyze and track?
<--- Score

26. What are the key input variables? What are the key process variables? What are the key output variables?
<--- Score

27. What is the quantifiable ROI for this solution (cost / time savings / data error minimization / etc)?
<--- Score

28. Do we offer real time analytics with big data and an sql support platform?
<--- Score

29. Avoiding Making Decisions in a Vacuum -- did the executive team set priorities with intimate contact with customers?

<--- Score

30. Do you aggressively reward and promote the people who have the biggest impact on creating excellent Azure Data Lake services/products?
<--- Score

31. Have changes been properly/adequately analyzed for effect?
<--- Score

32. Have you found any 'ground fruit' or 'low-hanging fruit' for immediate remedies to the gap in performance?
<--- Score

33. Do staff have the necessary skills to collect, analyze, and report data?
<--- Score

34. What are some innovative ways that data mining big data and data analysis could provide new and useful products?
<--- Score

35. What are the costs of reform?
<--- Score

36. Are losses documented, analyzed, and remedial processes developed to prevent future losses?
<--- Score

37. What methods are feasible and acceptable to estimate the impact of reforms?
<--- Score

38. Is key measure data collection planned and executed, process variation displayed and communicated and performance baselined?
<--- Score

39. How do you measure efficient delivery of Azure Data Lake services?
<--- Score

40. What is Advanced Analytics?
<--- Score

41. Are the units of measure consistent?
<--- Score

42. Does Azure Data Lake systematically track and analyze outcomes for accountability and quality improvement?
<--- Score

43. Are high impact defects defined and identified in the business process?
<--- Score

44. What are some interesting big data and analytics startups?
<--- Score

45. How do you focus on what is right -not who is right?
<--- Score

46. What are your customers expectations and measures?
<--- Score

47. How is the value delivered by Azure Data Lake being measured?
<--- Score

48. Is the solution cost-effective?
<--- Score

49. How large is the gap between current performance and the customer-specified (goal) performance?
<--- Score

50. Are the measurements objective?
<--- Score

51. Is Process Variation Displayed/Communicated?
<--- Score

52. Among the Azure Data Lake product and service cost to be estimated, which is considered hardest to estimate?
<--- Score

53. How do you aggregate measures across priorities?
<--- Score

54. What measurements are possible, practicable and meaningful?
<--- Score

55. Does your organization systematically track and analyze outcomes related for accountability and quality improvement?
<--- Score

56. How to cause the change?

<--- Score

57. How will you measure success?
<--- Score

58. How frequently do you track Azure Data Lake measures?
<--- Score

59. How do you measure lifecycle phases?
<--- Score

60. Who should receive measurement reports?
<--- Score

61. Not all analytic models are compatible with the Map/Reduce paradigm. How do you use big data to inform such models?
<--- Score

62. What would be a real cause for concern?
<--- Score

63. What harm might be caused?
<--- Score

64. Do you effectively measure and reward individual and team performance?
<--- Score

65. Is it possible to estimate the impact of unanticipated complexity such as wrong or failed assumptions, feedback, etc. on proposed reforms?
<--- Score

66. What causes mismanagement?

<--- Score

67. Can you measure the return on analysis?
<--- Score

68. What measurements are being captured?
<--- Score

69. Which stakeholder characteristics are analyzed?
<--- Score

70. How would you characterize the size of your data analysis problem?
<--- Score

71. What online courses would you recommend for someone looking to build their skills in analytics specifically big data?
<--- Score

72. How do you do risk analysis of rare, cascading, catastrophic events?
<--- Score

73. Was a data collection plan established?
<--- Score

74. Can controls strengthen the validity of decisions based on Big Data & Analytics by increasing the quality of the outcome?
<--- Score

75. Where do you do the analysis (that is, where do you run the tools/programs to analyze data)?
<--- Score

76. How do you stay flexible and focused to recognize larger Azure Data Lake results?
<--- Score

77. Have you made assumptions about the shape of the future, particularly its impact on your customers and competitors?
<--- Score

78. What is Big Data and Analytics?
<--- Score

79. You need to consolidate system logging for all of the clusters into a single location. The solution must provide near real-time analytics of the log data. What do you use?
<--- Score

80. Is a solid data collection plan established that includes measurement systems analysis?
<--- Score

81. What is measured? Why?
<--- Score

82. What are the agreed upon definitions of the high impact areas, defect(s), unit(s), and opportunities that will figure into the process capability metrics?
<--- Score

83. Why do the measurements/indicators matter?
<--- Score

84. What potential environmental factors impact the Azure Data Lake effort?
<--- Score

85. What is/are the corollaries for non-algorithmic analytics?

<--- Score

86. Are you aware of what could cause a problem?

<--- Score

87. Can the data be obtained at no cost, or is there a charge associated with access?

<--- Score

88. What causes innovation to fail or succeed in your organization?

<--- Score

89. How do we measure value of an analytic?

<--- Score

90. Overall cost (matrix, weighting, SVD, sims)?

<--- Score

91. Is data collection planned and executed?

<--- Score

92. How will measures be used to manage and adapt?

<--- Score

93. What disadvantage does this cause for the user?

<--- Score

94. Have the concerns of stakeholders to help identify and define potential barriers been obtained and analyzed?

<--- Score

95. How can you improve productivity in the analysis of big data?
<--- Score

96. How do you measure success?
<--- Score

97. What is new about big data and how does big data differ from traditional analytics?
<--- Score

98. Are there any easy-to-implement alternatives to Azure Data Lake? Sometimes other solutions are available that do not require the cost implications of a full-blown project?
<--- Score

99. How advanced will the data analysis procedures be?
<--- Score

100. What could cause you to change course?
<--- Score

101. What are your top 3 - 5 priorities for the quarter and how are you going to communicate them?
<--- Score

102. What is an unallowable cost?
<--- Score

103. Did you tackle the cause or the symptom?
<--- Score

104. Can you do Azure Data Lake without complex

(expensive) analysis?
<--- Score

105. How can you measure Azure Data Lake in a systematic way?
<--- Score

106. How are measurements made?
<--- Score

107. Who participated in the data collection for measurements?
<--- Score

108. What is the cost of partitioning/balancing?
<--- Score

109. What do you measure and why?
<--- Score

110. Are process variation components displayed/ communicated using suitable charts, graphs, plots?
<--- Score

111. Does Azure Data Lake analysis show the relationships among important Azure Data Lake factors?
<--- Score

112. Which measures and indicators matter?
<--- Score

113. Isnt big data just another way of saying analytics?
<--- Score

114. How will you measure your Azure Data Lake effectiveness?

<--- Score

115. Can analyses improve with better system and environment models?

<--- Score

116. What tools/programs do you use to analyze data?

<--- Score

117. Is the need persistent enough to justify development costs?

<--- Score

118. What has the team done to assure the stability and accuracy of the measurement process?

<--- Score

119. Does your organisation have the right analytical tools to handle (big) data?

<--- Score

120. How do you control the overall costs of your work processes?

<--- Score

121. What are your key Azure Data Lake organizational performance measures, including key short and longer-term financial measures?

<--- Score

122. How do you know that any Azure Data Lake analysis is complete and comprehensive?

<--- Score

123. Can analyses improve with more detailed analytics that we use?
<--- Score

124. You need to ensure that the support analysts can develop embedded analytics applications by using the least amount of development effort. Which technology do you implement?
<--- Score

125. Are there measurements based on task performance?
<--- Score

126. Where is it measured?
<--- Score

127. How will effects be measured?
<--- Score

128. How is progress measured?
<--- Score

129. What are the types and number of measures to use?
<--- Score

130. Is long term and short term variability accounted for?
<--- Score

131. Are you taking your company in the direction of better and revenue or cheaper and cost?
<--- Score

132. How can you measure the performance?
<--- Score

133. Have all non-recommended alternatives been analyzed in sufficient detail?
<--- Score

134. What relevant entities could be measured?
<--- Score

135. What languages, analysis, and tools/ technologies does your organization currently use or have experience with?
<--- Score

136. Is there a Performance Baseline?
<--- Score

137. What causes extra work or rework?
<--- Score

138. What are the best consulting firms specializing in big data analysis?
<--- Score

139. How do you maintain manual control over analytical algorithms and procedures?
<--- Score

140. What particular quality tools did the team find helpful in establishing measurements?
<--- Score

141. What data was collected (past, present, future/ ongoing)?
<--- Score

142. What is the right balance of time and resources between investigation, analysis, and discussion and dissemination?

<--- Score

143. The approach of traditional Azure Data Lake works for detail complexity but is focused on a systematic approach rather than an understanding of the nature of systems themselves, what approach will permit your organization to deal with the kind of unpredictable emergent behaviors that dynamic complexity can introduce?

<--- Score

144. How is performance measured?

<--- Score

145. What is the share of fixed costs in the total costs per vehicle?

<--- Score

146. For analysis use cases in big data what are the relative pros and cons of mpp dbmss versus hadoop other solutions?

<--- Score

147. How do you identify and analyze stakeholders and their interests?

<--- Score

148. How do your measurements capture actionable Azure Data Lake information for use in exceeding your customers expectations and securing your customers engagement?

<--- Score

149. What information do you want from the analytic process?

<--- Score

150. How will success or failure be measured?

<--- Score

151. How will your organization measure success?

<--- Score

152. How do you provide and measure performance?

<--- Score

153. What analytical tools do you consider particularly important?

<--- Score

154. How do you measure variability?

<--- Score

Add up total points for this section:
_ _ _ _ _ = Total points for this section

Divided by: _ _ _ _ _ _ (number of statements answered) = _ _ _ _ _ _
Average score for this section

Transfer your score to the Azure Data Lake Index at the beginning of the Self-Assessment.

CRITERION #4: ANALYZE:

INTENT: Analyze causes, assumptions and hypotheses.

In my belief, the answer to this question is clearly defined:

5 Strongly Agree

4 Agree

3 Neutral

2 Disagree

1 Strongly Disagree

1. How we make effective use of the flood of data that will be produced will be a real big data challenge: should we keep it all or could we throw some away?
<--- Score

2. What are new developments that are included in Big Data solutions?
<--- Score

3. What are your organizations drivers for using big data technologies and approaches?
<--- Score

4. Do all systems share a common Database Management System (DBMS) type?
<--- Score

5. What other organizational variables, such as reward systems or communication systems, affect the performance of this Azure Data Lake process?
<--- Score

6. What did the team gain from developing a sub-process map?
<--- Score

7. Do you, as a leader, bounce back quickly from setbacks?
<--- Score

8. Think about some of the processes you undertake within your organization, which do you own?
<--- Score

9. Is our data collection and acquisition optimized?
<--- Score

10. What will the naming convention be so that data sets can be easily discoverable by other business units?
<--- Score

11. What are your current levels and trends in key Azure Data Lake measures or indicators of product and process performance that are important to and

directly serve your customers?
<--- Score

12. How do you integrate with Data Governance programs?
<--- Score

13. A compounding model resolution with available relevant data can often provide insight towards a solution methodology; which Azure Data Lake models, tools and techniques are necessary?
<--- Score

14. Is data-driven decision-making part of the organisation's culture?
<--- Score

15. How are new Big Data developments captured in new Reference Architectures?
<--- Score

16. What is the right technique for distributing domains across processors?
<--- Score

17. How do you promote understanding that opportunity for improvement is not criticism of the status quo, or the people who created the status quo?
<--- Score

18. What are the main obstacles that prevent you from having access to all the datasets that are relevant for your organisation?
<--- Score

19. What were the financial benefits resulting from

any 'ground fruit or low-hanging fruit' (quick fixes)?
<--- Score

20. Quality vs. Quantity: What data are required to satisfy the given value proposition?
<--- Score

21. Do any programs address relevant technologies (e.g., web science, semantic web, big data technologies)?
<--- Score

22. Where did my data come from ?
<--- Score

23. What will drive Azure Data Lake change?
<--- Score

24. So how are managers using big data?
<--- Score

25. What are the main challenges in big data specifically hadoop related systems?
<--- Score

26. What if the data cannot fit on your computer?
<--- Score

27. How does Big Data enable predictive marketing?
<--- Score

28. In which area(s) do data integration and BI, as part of Fusion Middleware, help our IT infrastructure?
<--- Score

29. What is the limit for value as we add more data?
<--- Score

30. From what sources does your organisation collect, or expects to collect, data?
<--- Score

31. Is the Azure Data Lake process severely broken such that a re-design is necessary?
<--- Score

32. What about the nature of industrial data streams and the legacy automation equipment that is already out there?
<--- Score

33. How is your company organized to capture the beneit of big data and move swiftly to higher maturity stages?
<--- Score

34. What tool or practice do you find most effective in managing your Big Data?
<--- Score

35. What data is gathered?
<--- Score

36. What would be needed to support collaboration on data sharing across economic sectors?
<--- Score

37. Is Big data different?

<--- Score

38. You need a build a solution to ingest real-time streaming data into a nonrelational distributed database. What do you use to build the solution?
<--- Score

39. What are your Azure Data Lake processes?
<--- Score

40. How does Database as a Service make sense for an Enterprise like your organization?
<--- Score

41. Why is it that you are talking about data mining now?
<--- Score

42. What is your organizations process which leads to recognition of value generation?
<--- Score

43. Where is the data located?
<--- Score

44. What methods do you use to gather Azure Data Lake data?
<--- Score

45. What data is being licensed, and how or where is it being made available?
<--- Score

46. Are there any examples of big data paradigm being successfully used in demand forecasting?
<--- Score

47. What is next for big data applications?
<--- Score

48. What controls do you have in place to protect data?
<--- Score

49. Do you see specific areas that would benefit from increased interoperability (such as when the same work in areas like data transformation or data integration needs to be done over and over again or is very effort-intensive)?
<--- Score

50. What processes touched my data?
<--- Score

51. What is (or would be) the added value of collaborating with other entities regarding data sharing in your sector?
<--- Score

52. What does the data say about the performance of the business process?
<--- Score

53. What is the difference between data mining and big data in your oganization?
<--- Score

54. Do you have to transfer data as part of your application?
<--- Score

55. What are the revised rough estimates of the

financial savings/opportunity for Azure Data Lake improvements?

<--- Score

56. New roles. Executives interested in leading a big data transition can start with two simple techniques. First, they can get in the habit of asking "What do the data say?

<--- Score

57. What are the best opportunities for value improvement?

<--- Score

58. Are existing committees well placed to judge the ethical application of Big Data?

<--- Score

59. Have the problem and goal statements been updated to reflect the additional knowledge gained from the analyze phase?

<--- Score

60. Data Lake on NOSQL?

<--- Score

61. Is the required Azure Data Lake data gathered?

<--- Score

62. Is the process repeatable as we change algorithms and data structures?

<--- Score

63. Is your organisations business affected by regulatory restrictions on data/servers localisation requirements?

<--- Score

64. How to deal with too much data?
<--- Score

65. Which data stream mining tools can handle big data?
<--- Score

66. Are you ready for the era of big data?
<--- Score

67. Do your leaders quickly bounce back from setbacks?
<--- Score

68. How fresh does the data need to be?
<--- Score

69. Why is a search engine a Big Data application?
<--- Score

70. Do you see the need to support the development and implementation of technical solutions that are enhancing data protection 'by design' and 'by default'?
<--- Score

71. Have any additional benefits been identified that will result from closing all or most of the gaps?
<--- Score

72. Do your contracts/agreements contain data security obligations?
<--- Score

73. What is the next big thing after big data?
<--- Score

74. How should we organize to capture the benefit of Big Data and move swiftly to higher maturity stages?
<--- Score

75. Which systems are most and least susceptible to data quality issues?
<--- Score

76. What would be needed to support collaboration on data sharing in your sector?
<--- Score

77. Can good algorithms, models, heuristics overcome Data Quality problems?
<--- Score

78. What if the needle in the haystack happens to be a complex data structure?
<--- Score

79. What types of questions can Big Data help answer?
<--- Score

80. Are gaps between current performance and the goal performance identified?
<--- Score

81. Where value creation is one directional, what value do you create in the customer buying process?
<--- Score

82. Does your organisation perceive the need for more effort to promote security and trust in data technologies?
<--- Score

83. Does your organisation have the right tools to handle unstructured data expressed in natural language(s)?
<--- Score

84. How is the way you as the leader think and process information affecting your organizational culture?
<--- Score

85. What are the Big Data business problems you are now addressing – or will likely address soon?
<--- Score

86. Is big data good or bad for consumers?
<--- Score

87. Why does big data imply that more ssds will be sold due to greater throughput requirements of big data; are your big data projects really that dependent on speed?
<--- Score

88. What is the cost of poor quality as supported by the team's analysis?
<--- Score

89. Do you see a need to share data processing facilities?
<--- Score

90. When do you need a Data Governance practice?

<--- Score

91. In which field do you see the biggest chance for innovation and new businesses models due to big data and data mining?

<--- Score

92. Which industries capture the most value from big data?

<--- Score

93. What innovations will there be in big data over the next two years?

<--- Score

94. What are new applications that are enabled by Big Data solutions?

<--- Score

95. What successful thing are you doing today that may be blinding you to new growth opportunities?

<--- Score

96. Do several people in different organizational units assist with the Azure Data Lake process?

<--- Score

97. How will the DSS fit into the decision-making process?

<--- Score

98. Should we use data without the permission of individual owners, such as copying publicly available data?

<--- Score

99. How rigorous of a backup and recovery process will be required?
<--- Score

100. Were any designed experiments used to generate additional insight into the data analysis?
<--- Score

101. What are some of the big data challenges that quantum computing can solve?
<--- Score

102. In big data etl how many records are an acceptable loss?
<--- Score

103. Is the gap/opportunity displayed and communicated in financial terms?
<--- Score

104. Is the data secure?
<--- Score

105. How can you avoid big data?
<--- Score

106. How is the conceptual framework built in order to prevent a Data Lake from becoming a Data Swamp?
<--- Score

107. To what extent does your organisation have experience with big data and data-driven innovation (DDI)?

<--- Score

108. What are your current levels and trends in key measures or indicators of Azure Data Lake product and process performance that are important to and directly serve your customers? How do these results compare with the performance of your competitors and other organizations with similar offerings?
<--- Score

109. What is the contribution of subsets of the data to the problem solution?
<--- Score

110. Is recruitment of staff with strong data skills crucial?
<--- Score

111. How do you use Azure Data Lake data and information to support organizational decision making and innovation?
<--- Score

112. Is the suppliers process defined and controlled?
<--- Score

113. What are the constraints if any in making big data systems transactional?
<--- Score

114. Do you see regulatory restrictions on data/ servers localisation requirements as obstacles for data-driven innovation?
<--- Score

115. Does the current big data trend promises

more than it can actually deliver?

<--- Score

116. Where are the data located?

<--- Score

117. Do we address the daunting challenge of Big Data: how to make an easy use of highly diverse data and provide knowledge?

<--- Score

118. Erp versus big data are the two philosophies of information architecture consistent complementary or in conflict with each other?

<--- Score

119. Are you experiencing a big data bubble?

<--- Score

120. In the world of big data who are the experts and what are the companies in this space?

<--- Score

121. Identify an operational issue in your organization. for example, could a particular task be done more quickly or more efficiently by Azure Data Lake?

<--- Score

122. The use of the term big in Big Data evokes the idea that one is dealing with something large and formidable. But what exactly distinguishes big from small?

<--- Score

123. How much data might be lost to pruning?

<--- Score

124. How do you know whether a data mining solution is really needed?
<--- Score

125. Looking at Hadoop Big Data in the rearview mirror, what would you have done differently after implementing a data lake?
<--- Score

126. Do people think that big data is just a new buzzword for data mining?
<--- Score

127. What tangible benefits do you hope to achieve through your big data initiatives?
<--- Score

128. Your question to you is, are there any big data sets that are too big to fail?
<--- Score

129. How to visualize non-numeric data, e.g. text, icons, or images?
<--- Score

130. How do you separate the big data hype from the reality?
<--- Score

131. What attributes define Big Data solutions?
<--- Score

132. Where is Azure Data Lake data gathered?
<--- Score

133. What Is the Data's Governance ?
<--- Score

134. What is the difference between hadoop big data cassandra mongodb couchdb?
<--- Score

135. What are your key performance measures or indicators and in-process measures for the control and improvement of your Azure Data Lake processes?
<--- Score

136. What preprocessing do we need to do?
<--- Score

137. Can you add value to the current Azure Data Lake decision-making process (largely qualitative) by incorporating uncertainty modeling (more quantitative)?
<--- Score

138. How fast can we adapt to changes in the data stream?
<--- Score

139. What are the values at the data points?
<--- Score

140. Does your organisation have the necessary skills to handle big data?
<--- Score

141. Since there is no way to stop the accumulation of big data, should its use be regulated by the federal government?
<--- Score

142. Has your organization already invested in technology specifically designed to address the big data challenge?

<--- Score

143. In which area(s) do data integration and bi, as part of fusion middleware, help your it infrastructure?

<--- Score

144. What other jobs or tasks affect the performance of the steps in the Azure Data Lake process?

<--- Score

145. What rules and regulations should exist about combining data about individuals into a central repository?

<--- Score

146. What conclusions were drawn from the team's data collection and analysis? How did the team reach these conclusions?

<--- Score

147. Will data scientists live up to the expectations or will big data be a disappointment?

<--- Score

148. Are we collecting data once and using it many times, or duplicating data collection efforts and submerging data in silos?

<--- Score

149. Where did this data come from?

<--- Score

150. How is big data different from traditional data environments and related applications?

<--- Score

151. How is this data represented?

<--- Score

152. What are the most influential papers in the world of big data why?

<--- Score

153. Does your organisation buy datasets from other entities?

<--- Score

154. How can we summarize streaming data?

<--- Score

155. Who is collecting all this data?

<--- Score

156. What Is Data Governance ?

<--- Score

157. Are Azure Data Lake changes recognized early enough to be approved through the regular process?

<--- Score

158. Did any additional data need to be collected?

<--- Score

159. Is the performance gap determined?

<--- Score

160. Even when we have a lot of data, do we

understand it?
<--- Score

161. What about Volunteered data?
<--- Score

162. In your view, what can your roganization do to improve value creation from data-driven innovation?
<--- Score

163. Why a Data Lake?
<--- Score

164. How much data is really relevant to the problem solution?
<--- Score

165. What opportunities or data uses do you see from access to a rich/deep datasets?
<--- Score

166. Does Big Data Really Need HPC?
<--- Score

167. You need to automate the copying of the data to Azure Storage. Which tool do you use?
<--- Score

168. Will data miners and data scientist of big data be happy with a tool for data discovery and model building that is completely gui based i.e drag n drop workflow?
<--- Score

169. Can mapreduce be used for big hypothesis

instead of big data?

<--- Score

170. What tools do you consider particularly important to handle unstructured data expressed in natural language(s)?

<--- Score

171. What tools were used to generate the list of possible causes?

<--- Score

172. How much data so far?

<--- Score

173. How much data correction can we do at the edges?

<--- Score

174. Who will own and be responsible for tagging the data sets?

<--- Score

175. How should your organization use information systems big data to maximize performance?

<--- Score

176. How often will data be collected for measures?

<--- Score

177. Do you put data in a repository that might not be supported tomorrow?

<--- Score

178. What are the state of art clustering methods

for large or big data sets?
<--- Score

179. Is your organisation's business affected by regulatory restrictions on data/servers localisation requirements?
<--- Score

180. What tools were used to narrow the list of possible causes?
<--- Score

181. Does your organisation share data with other entities (with customers, suppliers, companies, government, etc)?
<--- Score

182. What is Big Data to us?
<--- Score

183. What type of data consumption do you support?
<--- Score

184. What types of data does your department use from external sources?
<--- Score

185. How do we track the provenance of the derived data/information?
<--- Score

186. To what extent does data-driven innovation add to the competitive advantage (CA) of your company?
<--- Score

187. What is (or would be) the added value of collaborating with other entities regarding data sharing across economic sectors?

<--- Score

188. How do you deal with very large data volumes and different varieties of data?

<--- Score

189. At what point is the data no longer necessary, if ever?

<--- Score

190. Where is the data coming from to measure compliance?

<--- Score

191. The format of the data is also important; what format will be used later in the data lake for processing?

<--- Score

192. What are the primary challenges and best practices for rolling out Big data projects?

<--- Score

193. Are there any further important challenges with respect to data-driven innovation in your organization where measures at national or state level should be put in place (please note: this does not only mean regulatory measures)?

<--- Score

194. How is Azure Data Lake data gathered?

<--- Score

195. Is big data indifferent to the semantic web i.e. linked data?

<--- Score

196. What quality tools were used to get through the analyze phase?

<--- Score

197. What are some interesting case studies involving big data?

<--- Score

198. Why are we collecting all this data?

<--- Score

199. Big data: Hype or helpful?

<--- Score

200. Were there any improvement opportunities identified from the process analysis?

<--- Score

201. Are traditional AI algorithms suitable for our big data projects?

<--- Score

202. Can we really afford to store and process all that data?

<--- Score

203. An organizationally feasible system request is one that considers the mission, goals and objectives of the organization. Key questions are: is the Azure Data Lake solution request practical and will it solve a problem or take advantage of an opportunity to

achieve company goals?
<--- Score

204. When choosing solutions for a big data deployment in a low latency environment what factors do you take into consideration?
<--- Score

205. What parts of the decision-making process will be supported by the system?
<--- Score

206. Was a detailed process map created to amplify critical steps of the 'as is' business process?
<--- Score

207. What are the ways in which cloud computing and big data can work together?
<--- Score

208. Do you see the need to clarify copyright aspects of the data-driven innovation (e.g. with respect to technologies such as text and data mining)?
<--- Score

209. How do you architect the system for Big Data?
<--- Score

210. In which way does big data create, or is expected to create, value in the organisation?
<--- Score

211. How do mission and objectives affect the Azure Data Lake processes of your organization?
<--- Score

212. How will big data transform policy management control?

<--- Score

213. How frequently will the data and product life cycles reset?

<--- Score

214. Can I connect this data to data I already have?

<--- Score

215. Do your employees have the opportunity to do what they do best everyday?

<--- Score

216. How to identify relevant fragments of data easily from a multitude of data sources?

<--- Score

217. Which file format should you use to receive the data?

<--- Score

218. How do your work systems and key work processes relate to and capitalize on your core competencies?

<--- Score

219. Where is search fitting in big data?

<--- Score

220. How does the organization define, manage, and improve its Azure Data Lake processes?

<--- Score

221. How was the detailed process map generated, verified, and validated?

<--- Score

222. What are your best practices for minimizing Azure Data Lake project risk, while demonstrating incremental value and quick wins throughout the Azure Data Lake project lifecycle?

<--- Score

223. Which statements about Big Data is true?

<--- Score

224. Which Oracle Data Integration products are used in your solution?

<--- Score

225. Was a cause-and-effect diagram used to explore the different types of causes (or sources of variation)?

<--- Score

226. From all the data collected by your organisation, what is approximately the percentage that is further processed for value generation?

<--- Score

227. What level of latency is your organization comfortable with in accessing the data for each type of function?

<--- Score

228. Do you have relations with organizations in terms of abilities to leverage big data in the supply chain?

<--- Score

229. What is collecting all this data?

<--- Score

230. How can you continue using your data?

<--- Score

231. How will your systems and methods evolve to remove Big Data solution weaknesses?

<--- Score

232. Are our Big Data investment programs results driven?

<--- Score

233. Were Pareto charts (or similar) used to portray the 'heavy hitters' (or key sources of variation)?

<--- Score

234. Who wants to store the data like this?

<--- Score

235. Do you see the need to address the issues of data "ownership" or access to non-personal data (e.g. machine-generated data)?

<--- Score

236. Technology Drivers – What were the primary technical challenges your organization faced?

<--- Score

237. Record-keeping requirements flow from the records needed as inputs, outputs, controls and for transformation of a Azure Data Lake process. Are the records needed as inputs to the Azure Data Lake process available?

<--- Score

238. Should we be required to inform individuals when we use their data?
<--- Score

239. What process should you select for improvement?
<--- Score

240. How is our sector leveraging the big data technologies?
<--- Score

241. From all data collected by your organisation, what is approximately the share of external data (collected from external sources), compared to internal data (produced by your operations)?
<--- Score

242. How do you implement and manage your work processes to ensure that they meet design requirements?
<--- Score

243. Have we let algorithms and large centralized data centres not only control the remembering but also the meaning and interpretation of the data?
<--- Score

244. What type(s) of data does your organisation find relevant but has not yet been able to exploit?
<--- Score

245. Is senior management in your organisation involved in big data-related projects?

<--- Score

246. Data governance: Does your organization have a data governance model, and how effective is data governance with the big data program?
<--- Score

247. How do you measure the operational performance of your key work systems and processes, including productivity, cycle time, and other appropriate measures of process effectiveness, efficiency, and innovation?
<--- Score

248. How much value is created for each unit of data (whatever it is)?
<--- Score

249. What (additional) data do these algorithms need to be effective?
<--- Score

250. What were the crucial 'moments of truth' on the process map?
<--- Score

251. How old is this data?
<--- Score

252. Are you considering open source options like Hadoop and new age architectures like data discovery platforms and data lakes?
<--- Score

253. Are we Using Data To Win?
<--- Score

254. What is it that we don't know we don't know about the data?

<--- Score

255. Did any value-added analysis or 'lean thinking' take place to identify some of the gaps shown on the 'as is' process map?

<--- Score

256. Is Big Data the right way to solve your problems?

<--- Score

257. Wheres the evidence that using big data intelligently will improve business performance?

<--- Score

258. Scope: To what extent does the big data program support all parts of your organization and all potential users?

<--- Score

259. Is Data and process analysis, root cause analysis and quantifying the gap/opportunity in place?

<--- Score

260. What Azure Data Lake data do you gather or use now?

<--- Score

261. How do you identify specific Azure Data Lake investment opportunities and emerging trends?

<--- Score

262. What can management do to improve value

creation from data-driven innovation?

<--- Score

263. Is data-driven decision-making part of the organisations culture?

<--- Score

264. Which control measures are appropriate for Big Data implementations, and based on a real-life business case study, what control measures have been applied and found effective?

<--- Score

265. How fast can we determine changes in the incoming data?

<--- Score

266. Think about the functions involved in your Azure Data Lake project, what processes flow from these functions?

<--- Score

267. What types of data ingestion pipelines do you have, at what frequency?

<--- Score

268. What are the primary business drivers for our initiative. What business challenges do we face?

<--- Score

269. Does our entire organization have easy access to information required to support work processes?

<--- Score

270. What is the Quality of the Result if the Quality

of the Data/Metadata is poor?
<--- Score

Add up total points for this section:
_____ = Total points for this section

Divided by: _____ (number of
statements answered) = _____
Average score for this section

Transfer your score to the Azure Data
Lake Index at the beginning of the Self-
Assessment.

CRITERION #5: IMPROVE:

INTENT: Develop a practical solution. Innovate, establish and test the solution and to measure the results.

In my belief, the answer to this question is clearly defined:

5 Strongly Agree

4 Agree

3 Neutral

2 Disagree

1 Strongly Disagree

1. What communications are necessary to support the implementation of the solution?
<--- Score

2. What is the team's contingency plan for potential problems occurring in implementation?
<--- Score

3. Are you assessing Azure Data Lake and risk?

<--- Score

4. How will the organization know that the solution worked?
<--- Score

5. Does the risk register include the real risks?
<--- Score

6. What should a proof of concept or pilot accomplish?
<--- Score

7. What is the role of government in workforce development?
<--- Score

8. What should you use to build the solution?
<--- Score

9. Is a contingency plan established?
<--- Score

10. Do you combine technical expertise with business knowledge and Azure Data Lake Key topics include lifecycles, development approaches, requirements and how to make a business case?
<--- Score

11. Is the measure of success for Azure Data Lake understandable to a variety of people?
<--- Score

12. To what extent does management recognize Azure Data Lake as a tool to increase the results?
<--- Score

13. Who will be responsible for documenting the Azure Data Lake requirements in detail?
<--- Score

14. What practices helps your organization to develop its capacity to recognize patterns?
<--- Score

15. How will you know that a change is an improvement?
<--- Score

16. What to do with the results or outcomes of measurements?
<--- Score

17. How do you improve your likelihood of success ?
<--- Score

18. What tools were used to evaluate the potential solutions?
<--- Score

19. Does the goal represent a desired result that can be measured?
<--- Score

20. How do you decide how much to remunerate an employee?
<--- Score

21. Which of the recognised risks out of all risks can be most likely transferred?
<--- Score

22. Who controls the risk?

<--- Score

23. Do we understand the public perception of our service delivery at any given time?

<--- Score

24. Solution for updating (i.e., adding documents)?

<--- Score

25. How risky is your organization?

<--- Score

26. How do you measure risk?

<--- Score

27. What tools do you use once you have decided on a Azure Data Lake strategy and more importantly how do you choose?

<--- Score

28. How do you improve productivity?

<--- Score

29. How will you know when its improved?

<--- Score

30. Explorations of the frontiers of Azure Data Lake will help you build influence, improve Azure Data Lake, optimize decision making, and sustain change, what is your approach?

<--- Score

31. Risk Identification: What are the possible risk events your organization faces in relation to Azure Data Lake?

<--- Score

32. How can you improve performance?
<--- Score

33. Is there a small-scale pilot for proposed improvement(s)? What conclusions were drawn from the outcomes of a pilot?
<--- Score

34. What were the underlying assumptions on the cost-benefit analysis?
<--- Score

35. Is there a cost/benefit analysis of optimal solution(s)?
<--- Score

36. How do you go about comparing Azure Data Lake approaches/solutions?
<--- Score

37. How will you know that you have improved?
<--- Score

38. What error proofing will be done to address some of the discrepancies observed in the 'as is' process?
<--- Score

39. For decision problems, how do you develop a decision statement?
<--- Score

40. Will the controls trigger any other risks?
<--- Score

41. Are possible solutions generated and tested?
<--- Score

42. How does the solution remove the key sources of issues discovered in the analyze phase?
<--- Score

43. What lessons, if any, from a pilot were incorporated into the design of the full-scale solution?
<--- Score

44. Are the best solutions selected?
<--- Score

45. Can you identify any significant risks or exposures to Azure Data Lake third- parties (vendors, service providers, alliance partners etc) that concern you?
<--- Score

46. Was a pilot designed for the proposed solution(s)?
<--- Score

47. How do you mitigate the risks associated with digital disruption?
<--- Score

48. How long will the development phase take time?
<--- Score

49. At what point will vulnerability assessments be performed once Azure Data Lake is put into production (e.g., ongoing Risk Management after implementation)?
<--- Score

50. If you could make changes to any of the top risk systems, what changes would you propose?
<--- Score

51. Is the implementation plan designed?
<--- Score

52. How will you measure the results?
<--- Score

53. How do the Azure Data Lake results compare with the performance of your competitors and other organizations with similar offerings?
<--- Score

54. What tools were most useful during the improve phase?
<--- Score

55. Are risk triggers captured?
<--- Score

56. What is the Azure Data Lake's sustainability risk?
<--- Score

57. Do you get the same results from the different sources?
<--- Score

58. What is the magnitude of the improvements?
<--- Score

59. Is supporting Azure Data Lake documentation required?
<--- Score

60. How can skill-level changes improve Azure Data Lake?
<--- Score

61. How do you link measurement and risk?
<--- Score

62. What resources are required for the improvement efforts?
<--- Score

63. Which other Oracle products are used in your solution?
<--- Score

64. Describe the design of the pilot and what tests were conducted, if any?
<--- Score

65. Are there any constraints (technical, political, cultural, or otherwise) that would inhibit certain solutions?
<--- Score

66. If you could go back in time five years, what decision would you make differently? What is your best guess as to what decision you're making today you might regret five years from now?
<--- Score

67. What can you do to improve?
<--- Score

68. Is a solution implementation plan established, including schedule/work breakdown structure, resources, risk management plan, cost/budget, and

control plan?

<--- Score

69. How do you keep improving Azure Data Lake?

<--- Score

70. Have you identified breakpoints and/or risk tolerances that will trigger broad consideration of a potential need for intervention or modification of strategy?

<--- Score

71. What metrics do we use to assess the results?

<--- Score

72. Is pilot data collected and analyzed?

<--- Score

73. In the past few months, what is the smallest change you have made that has had the biggest positive result? What was it about that small change that produced the large return?

<--- Score

74. Hybrid partitioning (across rows/terms and columns/documents) useful?

<--- Score

75. How do you improve Azure Data Lake service perception, and satisfaction?

<--- Score

76. When you map the key players in your own work and the types/domains of relationships with them, which relationships do you find easy and which challenging, and why?

<--- Score

77. Risk events: what are the things that could go wrong?
<--- Score

78. What tools were used to tap into the creativity and encourage 'outside the box' thinking?
<--- Score

79. Why improve in the first place?
<--- Score

80. How do you manage and improve your Azure Data Lake work systems to deliver customer value and achieve organizational success and sustainability?
<--- Score

81. How will the team or the process owner(s) monitor the implementation plan to see that it is working as intended?
<--- Score

82. What does the 'should be' process map/design look like?
<--- Score

83. Do those selected for the Azure Data Lake team have a good general understanding of what Azure Data Lake is all about?
<--- Score

84. How can you improve Azure Data Lake?
<--- Score

85. For estimation problems, how do you develop an

estimation statement?
<--- Score

86. Is the solution technically practical?
<--- Score

87. Who controls key decisions that will be made?
<--- Score

88. What is Azure Data Lake's impact on utilizing the best solution(s)?
<--- Score

89. What attendant changes will need to be made to ensure that the solution is successful?
<--- Score

90. How do you improve cross-organizational information sharing for broader connected intelligence?
<--- Score

91. Are improved process ('should be') maps modified based on pilot data and analysis?
<--- Score

92. How do you measure progress and evaluate training effectiveness?
<--- Score

93. What actually has to improve and by how much?
<--- Score

94. Is the scope clearly documented?
<--- Score

95. How do you define the solutions' scope?
<--- Score

96. Who will be using the results of the measurement activities?
<--- Score

97. What improvements have been achieved?
<--- Score

98. Is there a high likelihood that any recommendations will achieve their intended results?
<--- Score

99. What is the risk?
<--- Score

100. Is this a brand new solution, or are you augmenting an existing solution?
<--- Score

101. MapReduce: forgotten?
<--- Score

102. How does the team improve its work?
<--- Score

103. Do you see areas in your domain or across domains where vendor lock-in is a potential risk?
<--- Score

104. How robust are the results?
<--- Score

105. What are the implications of the one critical Azure Data Lake decision 10 minutes, 10 months, and

10 years from now?

<--- Score

106. Who will be responsible for making the decisions to include or exclude requested changes once Azure Data Lake is underway?

<--- Score

107. Can the solution be designed and implemented within an acceptable time period?

<--- Score

108. What are your current levels and trends in key measures or indicators of workforce and leader development?

<--- Score

109. Is the optimal solution selected based on testing and analysis?

<--- Score

110. What is the implementation plan?

<--- Score

111. Do we understand the mechanisms and patterns that underlie transportation in our jurisdiction?

<--- Score

112. How do you measure improved Azure Data Lake service perception, and satisfaction?

<--- Score

113. Risk factors: what are the characteristics of Azure Data Lake that make it risky?

<--- Score

114. Are new and improved process ('should be') maps developed?
<--- Score

115. Do we understand public perception of transportation service delivery at any given time?
<--- Score

116. Who are the people involved in developing and implementing Azure Data Lake?
<--- Score

117. How did the team generate the list of possible solutions?
<--- Score

118. How significant is the improvement in the eyes of the end user?
<--- Score

119. Were any criteria developed to assist the team in testing and evaluating potential solutions?
<--- Score

120. What went well, what should change, what can improve?
<--- Score

121. What needs improvement? Why?
<--- Score

122. What decisions need support?
<--- Score

123. What do you want to improve?

<--- Score

Add up total points for this section:
_ _ _ _ _ = Total points for this section

Divided by: _ _ _ _ _ _ (number of
statements answered) = _ _ _ _ _ _
Average score for this section

Transfer your score to the Azure Data
Lake Index at the beginning of the Self-
Assessment.

CRITERION #6: CONTROL:

INTENT: Implement the practical solution. Maintain the performance and correct possible complications.

In my belief, the answer to this question is clearly defined:

5 Strongly Agree

4 Agree

3 Neutral

2 Disagree

1 Strongly Disagree

1. How will input, process, and output variables be checked to detect for sub-optimal conditions?
<--- Score

2. How do you establish and deploy modified action plans if circumstances require a shift in plans and rapid execution of new plans?
<--- Score

3. Where do ideas that reach policy makers and planners as proposals for Azure Data Lake strengthening and reform actually originate?
<--- Score

4. Is a response plan established and deployed?
<--- Score

5. Is knowledge gained on process shared and institutionalized?
<--- Score

6. Is there documentation that will support the successful operation of the improvement?
<--- Score

7. What are the key elements of your Azure Data Lake performance improvement system, including your evaluation, organizational learning, and innovation processes?
<--- Score

8. Are pertinent alerts monitored, analyzed and distributed to appropriate personnel?
<--- Score

9. Are controls in place and consistently applied?
<--- Score

10. Are suggested corrective/restorative actions indicated on the response plan for known causes to problems that might surface?
<--- Score

11. Have new or revised work instructions resulted?
<--- Score

12. Are documented procedures clear and easy to follow for the operators?
<--- Score

13. What other areas of the organization might benefit from the Azure Data Lake team's improvements, knowledge, and learning?
<--- Score

14. Is there a transfer of ownership and knowledge to process owner and process team tasked with the responsibilities.
<--- Score

15. Are you measuring, monitoring and predicting Azure Data Lake activities to optimize operations and profitability, and enhancing outcomes?
<--- Score

16. Who will be in control?
<--- Score

17. Will your goals reflect your program budget?
<--- Score

18. What do you measure to verify effectiveness gains?
<--- Score

19. Is the range of stakeholder goals and values identified and reflected?
<--- Score

20. How will you measure your QA plan's effectiveness?

<--- Score

21. Are the planned controls working?
<--- Score

22. Is there a standardized process?
<--- Score

23. What quality tools were useful in the control phase?
<--- Score

24. What do you stand for--and what are you against?
<--- Score

25. What are standard ruby on rails solutions for using data mining and big data oriented non mysql sql and nosql data stores?
<--- Score

26. Is there a documented and implemented monitoring plan?
<--- Score

27. Future Plans - What is the future plan to expand this solution?
<--- Score

28. Do you see the need for actions in the area of standardisation (including both formal standards and the promotion of/agreement on de facto standards) related to your sector?
<--- Score

29. How might the organization capture best practices and lessons learned so as to leverage improvements

across the business?

<--- Score

30. How will the process owner and team be able to hold the gains?

<--- Score

31. Act/Adjust: What Do you Need to Do Differently?

<--- Score

32. In which context do you see the need for standardisation actions?

<--- Score

33. Who has control over resources?

<--- Score

34. How likely is the current Azure Data Lake plan to come in on schedule or on budget?

<--- Score

35. How do your controls stack up?

<--- Score

36. What organization security and data governance standards will apply for the data collected?

<--- Score

37. Is there a recommended audit plan for routine surveillance inspections of Azure Data Lake's gains?

<--- Score

38. Where do you see the need for standardisation actions?

<--- Score

39. What is the control/monitoring plan?
<--- Score

40. At which levels do you see the need for standardisation actions?
<--- Score

41. How do senior leaders actions reflect a commitment to the organizations Azure Data Lake values?
<--- Score

42. How will new or emerging customer needs/requirements be checked/communicated to orient the process toward meeting the new specifications and continually reducing variation?
<--- Score

43. Is there a test environment that you can play around in to learn mapreduce and implement hdfs hive hbase and other big data system on a data store?
<--- Score

44. Are operating procedures consistent?
<--- Score

45. Implementation Planning: is a pilot needed to test the changes before a full roll out occurs?
<--- Score

46. Who sets the Azure Data Lake standards?
<--- Score

47. Is reporting being used or needed?

<--- Score

48. Who is the Azure Data Lake process owner?
<--- Score

49. What is your theory of human motivation, and how does your compensation plan fit with that view?
<--- Score

50. How do you plan on providing proper recognition and disclosure of supporting companies?
<--- Score

51. Does Azure Data Lake appropriately measure and monitor risk?
<--- Score

52. Is new knowledge gained imbedded in the response plan?
<--- Score

53. Where does your organization plan on hosting the data - locally or in the cloud?
<--- Score

54. How will report readings be checked to effectively monitor performance?
<--- Score

55. What adjustments to the strategies are needed?
<--- Score

56. Can you adapt and adjust to changing Azure Data Lake situations?
<--- Score

57. What should the next improvement project be that is related to Azure Data Lake?
<--- Score

58. What are your results for key measures or indicators of the accomplishment of your Azure Data Lake strategy and action plans, including building and strengthening core competencies?
<--- Score

59. What do your reports reflect?
<--- Score

60. How will the day-to-day responsibilities for monitoring and continual improvement be transferred from the improvement team to the process owner?
<--- Score

61. What is the recommended frequency of auditing?
<--- Score

62. When we plan and design, how well do we capture previous experience?
<--- Score

63. Does job training on the documented procedures need to be part of the process team's education and training?
<--- Score

64. Is a response plan in place for when the input, process, or output measures indicate an 'out-of-control' condition?
<--- Score

65. What problems can be solved using machine learning where a problem data size is such that it will require big data skills to implement?
<--- Score

66. What is the best design framework for Azure Data Lake organization now that, in a post industrial-age if the top-down, command and control model is no longer relevant?
<--- Score

67. You plan to copy data from Azure Blob storage to an Azure SQL database by using Azure Data Factory. Which file formats do you use?
<--- Score

68. Do you monitor the Azure Data Lake decisions made and fine tune them as they evolve?
<--- Score

69. What can you control?
<--- Score

70. What are some strategies for capacity planning for big data processing and cloud computing?
<--- Score

71. How can you best use all of your knowledge repositories to enhance learning and sharing?
<--- Score

72. In the case of a Azure Data Lake project, the criteria for the audit derive from implementation objectives. an audit of a Azure Data Lake project involves assessing whether the recommendations outlined for implementation have been met. Can you

track that any Azure Data Lake project is implemented as planned, and is it working?
<--- Score

73. What are you attempting to measure/monitor?
<--- Score

74. How will the process owner verify improvement in present and future sigma levels, process capabilities?
<--- Score

75. Does the Azure Data Lake performance meet the customer's requirements?
<--- Score

76. What key inputs and outputs are being measured on an ongoing basis?
<--- Score

77. Will the team be available to assist members in planning investigations?
<--- Score

78. Will any special training be provided for results interpretation?
<--- Score

79. Do the Azure Data Lake decisions you make today help people and the planet tomorrow?
<--- Score

80. Is learning hadoop and big data a good career path or fast getting commoditized?
<--- Score

81. Do you monitor the effectiveness of your Azure

Data Lake activities?
<--- Score

82. What other systems, operations, processes, and infrastructures (hiring practices, staffing, training, incentives/rewards, metrics/dashboards/scorecards, etc.) need updates, additions, changes, or deletions in order to facilitate knowledge transfer and improvements?
<--- Score

83. What should you measure to verify efficiency gains?
<--- Score

84. Can support from partners be adjusted?
<--- Score

85. How is change control managed?
<--- Score

86. What would be a great and prospective startup idea relating to machine learning augmented reality or big data or a combination of all three?
<--- Score

87. Which consulting firm has the best sophisticated algorithm big data high volume transactions machine learning ai practice?
<--- Score

88. How do you select, collect, align, and integrate Azure Data Lake data and information for tracking daily operations and overall organizational performance, including progress relative to strategic objectives and action plans?

<--- Score

89. How do you encourage people to take control and responsibility?
<--- Score

90. Does the response plan contain a definite closed loop continual improvement scheme (e.g., plan-do-check-act)?
<--- Score

91. Are there documented procedures?
<--- Score

92. How do controls support value?
<--- Score

93. Against what alternative is success being measured?
<--- Score

94. Who controls critical resources?
<--- Score

95. Is there a Azure Data Lake Communication plan covering who needs to get what information when?
<--- Score

96. Are new process steps, standards, and documentation ingrained into normal operations?
<--- Score

97. Does a troubleshooting guide exist or is it needed?
<--- Score

98. What are the known security controls?

<--- Score

99. Is there a control plan in place for sustaining improvements (short and long-term)?
<--- Score

100. How do you defend against the weakest link in your trusted, on-premises network?
<--- Score

101. What are the critical parameters to watch?
<--- Score

102. Has the improved process and its steps been standardized?
<--- Score

103. Are the planned controls in place?
<--- Score

104. You may have created your quality measures at a time when you lacked resources, technology wasn't up to the required standard, or low service levels were the industry norm. Have those circumstances changed?
<--- Score

Add up total points for this section:
_ _ _ _ _ = Total points for this section

Divided by: _ _ _ _ _ _ (number of statements answered) = _ _ _ _ _ _
Average score for this section

Transfer your score to the Azure Data Lake Index at the beginning of the Self-

Assessment.

CRITERION #7: SUSTAIN:

INTENT: Retain the benefits.

In my belief, the answer to this question is clearly defined:

5 Strongly Agree

4 Agree

3 Neutral

2 Disagree

1 Strongly Disagree

1. Who will be responsible for deciding whether Azure Data Lake goes ahead or not after the initial investigations?
<--- Score

2. Can you maintain your growth without detracting from the factors that have contributed to your success?
<--- Score

3. Who is responsible for ensuring appropriate

resources (time, people and money) are allocated to Azure Data Lake?
<--- Score

4. What are the usability implications of Azure Data Lake actions?
<--- Score

5. How do you lead with Azure Data Lake in mind?
<--- Score

6. Whose voice (department, ethnic group, women, older workers, etc) might you have missed hearing from in your company, and how might you amplify this voice to create positive momentum for your business?
<--- Score

7. Who uses your product in ways you never expected?
<--- Score

8. What would you recommend your friend do if he/she were facing this dilemma?
<--- Score

9. Would you rather sell to knowledgeable and informed customers or to uninformed customers?
<--- Score

10. Are your responses positive or negative?
<--- Score

11. Who is on the team?
<--- Score

12. Which systems do you or your group / department maintain?

<--- Score

13. How does that compare to other science disciplines?

<--- Score

14. What are the different types of references?

<--- Score

15. How does co-creation and personalization work from a content perspective?

<--- Score

16. How do you keep moving forward?

<--- Score

17. If there were zero limitations, what would you do differently?

<--- Score

18. Can you have a system that watches the server log les and raise service tickets automatically when the resource utilization crosses the threshold limit?

<--- Score

19. Why is it important to have senior management support for a Azure Data Lake project?

<--- Score

20. Should you change your medication?

<--- Score

21. What should you configure?

<--- Score

22. Are you maintaining a past–present–future perspective throughout the Azure Data Lake discussion?
<--- Score

23. What is it like to work for you?
<--- Score

24. What potential megatrends could make your business model obsolete?
<--- Score

25. What trouble can you get into?
<--- Score

26. If you weren't already in this business, would you enter it today? And if not, what are you going to do about it?
<--- Score

27. What are the benefits and drawbacks?
<--- Score

28. Is your strategy driving your strategy? Or is the way in which you allocate resources driving your strategy?
<--- Score

29. What would have to be true for the option on the table to be the best possible choice?
<--- Score

30. What knowledge, skills and characteristics mark a good Azure Data Lake project manager?

<--- Score

31. Can you do all this work?
<--- Score

32. How do you foster innovation?
<--- Score

33. How do I get to there from here?
<--- Score

34. How do you secure and govern it?
<--- Score

35. How do you maintain governance in a self-service, on-demand model?
<--- Score

36. What are we missing?
<--- Score

37. Who else should you help?
<--- Score

38. Do you have sufficient infrastructure to create full-test indexes for billions of files to support full discovery?
<--- Score

39. How to deal with ambiguity?
<--- Score

40. And the best indications from your own intel?
<--- Score

41. What may be the consequences for the

performance of an organization if all stakeholders are not consulted regarding Azure Data Lake?
<--- Score

42. How will you ensure you get what you expected?
<--- Score

43. Is Azure Data Lake realistic, or are you setting yourself up for failure?
<--- Score

44. What are you challenging?
<--- Score

45. Where are the tools available?
<--- Score

46. If you had to leave your organization for a year and the only communication you could have with employees/colleagues was a single paragraph, what would you write?
<--- Score

47. How does Azure Data Lake integrate with other business initiatives?
<--- Score

48. When information truly is ubiquitous, when reach and connectivity are completely global, when computing resources are infinite, and when a whole new set of impossibilities are not only possible, but happening, what will that do to your business?
<--- Score

49. What are your personal philosophies regarding Azure Data Lake and how do they influence your

work?
<--- Score

50. Are the criteria for selecting recommendations stated?
<--- Score

51. In the past year, what have you done (or could you have done) to increase the accurate perception of your company/brand as ethical and honest?
<--- Score

52. Is the Azure Data Lake organization completing tasks effectively and efficiently?
<--- Score

53. What are the business goals Azure Data Lake is aiming to achieve?
<--- Score

54. What should you stop doing?
<--- Score

55. How long will it take to change?
<--- Score

56. Who would you most like to hear from?
<--- Score

57. What is the role of government in research?
<--- Score

58. Who are four people whose careers you have enhanced?
<--- Score

59. Are all our algorithms covered by templates?
<--- Score

60. Who will provide the final approval of Azure Data Lake deliverables?
<--- Score

61. What threat is Azure Data Lake addressing?
<--- Score

62. How do you determine the key elements that affect Azure Data Lake workforce satisfaction, how are these elements determined for different workforce groups and segments?
<--- Score

63. Which Azure Data Lake goals are the most important?
<--- Score

64. Is it redundant?
<--- Score

65. If you do not follow, then how to lead?
<--- Score

66. What is effective Azure Data Lake?
<--- Score

67. Do you have the right capabilities and capacities?
<--- Score

68. How much does Azure Data Lake help?
<--- Score

69. What are you trying to prove to yourself, and how

might it be hijacking your life and business success?
<--- Score

70. Enterprise-level security based on Active Directory must be supported. What do you create?
<--- Score

71. Can you break it down?
<--- Score

72. Do you feel that more should be done in the Azure Data Lake area?
<--- Score

73. Can we realistically store everything?
<--- Score

74. Is there any existing Azure Data Lake governance structure?
<--- Score

75. Putting the customer at the center of attention, is that the basis of your marketing approach?
<--- Score

76. What goals did you miss?
<--- Score

77. Did it get exported, when, where how will it be used (organizational)?
<--- Score

78. Are you making progress, and are you making progress as Azure Data Lake leaders?
<--- Score

79. What is the expected user experience for organization operators?
<--- Score

80. Where can you break convention?
<--- Score

81. Are there any disadvantages to implementing Azure Data Lake? There might be some that are less obvious?
<--- Score

82. Whom among your colleagues do you trust, and for what?
<--- Score

83. Is Azure Data Lake dependent on the successful delivery of a current project?
<--- Score

84. What is the kind of project structure that would be appropriate for your Azure Data Lake project, should it be formal and complex, or can it be less formal and relatively simple?
<--- Score

85. Based on the experience with your implementation, would you participate in customer reference activities?
<--- Score

86. How do you deal with Azure Data Lake changes?
<--- Score

87. What kind of crime could a potential new hire have committed that would not only not disqualify

him/her from being hired by your organization, but would actually indicate that he/she might be a particularly good fit?

<--- Score

88. What does success looks like?

<--- Score

89. Were lessons learned captured and communicated?

<--- Score

90. Have benefits been optimized with all key stakeholders?

<--- Score

91. Have new benefits been realized?

<--- Score

92. Continuous Delivery – Is it right for you?

<--- Score

93. Do you have an implicit bias for capital investments over people investments?

<--- Score

94. Will it be accepted by users?

<--- Score

95. How do you proactively clarify deliverables and Azure Data Lake quality expectations?

<--- Score

96. How can you negotiate Azure Data Lake successfully with a stubborn boss, an irate client, or a deceitful coworker?

<--- Score

97. Which Oracle applications are used in your project?
<--- Score

98. Classification versus clustering?
<--- Score

99. What happens at your organization when people fail?
<--- Score

100. What is your question? Why?
<--- Score

101. What does the communication do?
<--- Score

102. What contribution does it make to business success?
<--- Score

103. How do you gain consumers trust?
<--- Score

104. What are the top 3 things at the forefront of your Azure Data Lake agendas for the next 3 years?
<--- Score

105. What is the craziest thing you can do?
<--- Score

106. Why use expensive machines when cheap ones suffice?
<--- Score

107. Are there any activities that you can take off your to do list?

<--- Score

108. How is implementation research currently incorporated into each of your goals?

<--- Score

109. Which individuals, teams or departments will be involved in Azure Data Lake?

<--- Score

110. Why is knowledge management important?

<--- Score

111. What are the key enablers to make this Azure Data Lake move?

<--- Score

112. Who are the key stakeholders?

<--- Score

113. At what level of maturity would you classify your organizations technical capabilities?

<--- Score

114. What did you miss in the interview for the worst hire you ever made?

<--- Score

115. What is your formula for success in Azure Data Lake ?

<--- Score

116. How to use in practice?

<--- Score

117. Is there a work around that you can use?
<--- Score

118. Where is the ROI?
<--- Score

119. If you find that you havent accomplished one of the goals for one of the steps of the Azure Data Lake strategy, what will you do to fix it?
<--- Score

120. What is an unauthorized commitment?
<--- Score

121. Classification versus regression?
<--- Score

122. Do you have a filter through which you put customer suggestions?
<--- Score

123. Ask yourself: how would you do this work if you only had one staff member to do it?
<--- Score

124. Playing to Win -- were you generally playing defense and have now gone of the offensive?
<--- Score

125. Why will customers want to buy your organizations products/services?
<--- Score

126. Which models, tools and techniques are

necessary?
<--- Score

127. Why Value Co-creation?
<--- Score

128. How do you determine what an item is about?
<--- Score

129. What do we do when new problems arise?
<--- Score

130. Who will determine interim and final deadlines?
<--- Score

131. In retrospect, of the projects that you pulled the plug on, what percent do you wish had been allowed to keep going, and what percent do you wish had ended earlier?
<--- Score

132. How are advances in digital technology changing the way you work, your industry and your community?
<--- Score

133. What is limiting the task?
<--- Score

134. Did your employees make progress today?
<--- Score

135. Which tool should you use?
<--- Score

136. Is the impact that Azure Data Lake has shown?

<--- Score

137. How are you doing compared to your industry?
<--- Score

138. Does your organization embrace technology and innovation?
<--- Score

139. What goals must be served by whatever action is taken?
<--- Score

140. Is it economical; do you have the time and money?
<--- Score

141. Does the in situ hardware have the computational capacity to support such algorithms?
<--- Score

142. How do you assess the Azure Data Lake pitfalls that are inherent in implementing it?
<--- Score

143. Are you paying enough attention to the partners your company depends on to succeed?
<--- Score

144. Who will manage the integration of tools?
<--- Score

145. In a project to restructure Azure Data Lake outcomes, which stakeholders would you involve?
<--- Score

146. Is your basic point _____ or _____?
<--- Score

147. Who, on the executive team or the board, has spoken to a customer recently?
<--- Score

148. How do you stay inspired?
<--- Score

149. How do you propose your organization request Key Management services?
<--- Score

150. What is your BATNA (best alternative to a negotiated agreement)?
<--- Score

151. What does your signature ensure?
<--- Score

152. How likely is it that a customer would recommend your company to a friend or colleague?
<--- Score

153. Who do you think the world wants your organization to be?
<--- Score

154. What you are going to do to affect the numbers?
<--- Score

155. What are specific Azure Data Lake rules to follow?
<--- Score

156. What must you excel at?
<--- Score

157. Why do and why don't your customers like your organization?
<--- Score

158. Did you have something to introduce into the record?
<--- Score

159. What is a feasible sequencing of reform initiatives over time?
<--- Score

160. Are you changing as fast as the world around you?
<--- Score

161. How much contingency will be available in the budget?
<--- Score

162. What load balancing technique should we use?
<--- Score

163. Has implementation been effective in reaching specified objectives so far?
<--- Score

164. How important is Azure Data Lake to the user organizations mission?
<--- Score

165. What projects are going on in the organization

today, and what resources are those projects using from the resource pools?
<--- Score

166. Are you relevant? Will you be relevant five years from now? Ten?
<--- Score

167. Do you have the right people on the bus?
<--- Score

168. Find traffic bottlenecks ?
<--- Score

169. What happens if you do not have enough funding?
<--- Score

170. Operational - will it work?
<--- Score

171. What are the success criteria that will indicate that Azure Data Lake objectives have been met and the benefits delivered?
<--- Score

172. What is your Azure Data Lake strategy?
<--- Score

173. How do you make it meaningful in connecting Azure Data Lake with what users do day-to-day?
<--- Score

174. Do you think you know, or do you know you know ?
<--- Score

175. Are you willing to go all the way to deliver on a specific brand promise; and are you willing to do something that appears customer unfriendly to help fund it?

<--- Score

176. Do you use any tools for workflow management?

<--- Score

177. What relationships among Azure Data Lake trends do you perceive?

<--- Score

178. How do you foster the skills, knowledge, talents, attributes, and characteristics you want to have?

<--- Score

179. Are you using a design thinking approach and integrating Innovation, Azure Data Lake Experience, and Brand Value?

<--- Score

180. Are our business activities mainly conducted in one country?

<--- Score

181. What can it be used for?

<--- Score

182. Are the assumptions believable and achievable?

<--- Score

183. How do you find out how your customers perceive the value of what you sell?

<--- Score

184. More efficient all-to-all operations (similarities)?

<--- Score

185. Which file formats can you use?

<--- Score

186. Is a Azure Data Lake team work effort in place?

<--- Score

187. What is the range of capabilities?

<--- Score

188. What kind of projects are expected in the future?

<--- Score

189. What are the essentials of internal Azure Data Lake management?

<--- Score

190. How do you ensure that implementations of Azure Data Lake products are done in a way that ensures safety?

<--- Score

191. What are internal and external Azure Data Lake relations?

<--- Score

192. What are current Azure Data Lake paradigms?

<--- Score

193. How fast can we affect the environment based

on what we see?
<--- Score

194. What are the gaps in your knowledge and experience?
<--- Score

195. What's limiting the task?
<--- Score

196. How do you manage Azure Data Lake Knowledge Management (KM)?
<--- Score

197. Who is responsible for Azure Data Lake?
<--- Score

198. Instead of going to current contacts for new ideas, what if you reconnected with dormant contacts--the people you used to know? If you were going reactivate a dormant tie, who would it be?
<--- Score

199. What Azure Data Lake modifications can you make work for you?
<--- Score

200. What is the purpose of Azure Data Lake in relation to the mission?
<--- Score

201. What is going to happen if the prosumer disappears?
<--- Score

202. If you got fired and a new hire took your place,

what would she do different?

<--- Score

203. What are strategies for increasing support and reducing opposition?

<--- Score

204. What are the benefits of using CSV or CSR?

<--- Score

205. Is maximizing Azure Data Lake protection the same as minimizing Azure Data Lake loss?

<--- Score

206. What current systems have to be understood and/or changed?

<--- Score

207. How do you cross-sell and up-sell your Azure Data Lake success?

<--- Score

208. What business challenges did you face?

<--- Score

209. What is the environment?

<--- Score

210. How do you engage the workforce, in addition to satisfying them?

<--- Score

211. What is knowledge management?

<--- Score

212. Do you know what you are doing? And who do

you call if you don't?

<--- Score

213. Can a organization get to know it is customers better?

<--- Score

214. How does the location of a point relate to its value?

<--- Score

215. How do you know that it is rigorous enough to feed every mind appropriately?

<--- Score

216. What key disruptive technologies or business models do you see?

<--- Score

217. What business benefits will Azure Data Lake goals deliver if achieved?

<--- Score

218. Hash tables for term management?

<--- Score

219. What is the recommended frequency of auditing?

<--- Score

220. Which technology should you implement?

<--- Score

221. Are you / should you be revolutionary or evolutionary?

<--- Score

222. How do you track customer value, profitability or financial return, organizational success, and sustainability?
<--- Score

223. What have you done to protect your business from competitive encroachment?
<--- Score

224. Who have you, as a company, historically been when you've been at your best?
<--- Score

225. What is something you believe that nearly no one agrees with you on?
<--- Score

226. What new services of functionality will be implemented next with Azure Data Lake ?
<--- Score

227. How strict to be with dimensional design?
<--- Score

228. Why is Azure Data Lake important for you now?
<--- Score

229. How do you listen to customers to obtain actionable information?
<--- Score

230. How do you know if you are successful?
<--- Score

231. Are you satisfied with your current role? If not, what is missing from it?

<--- Score

232. How will this affect the marketing of companies?

<--- Score

233. What will be the consequences to the stakeholder (financial, reputation etc) if Azure Data Lake does not go ahead or fails to deliver the objectives?

<--- Score

234. What are the short and long-term Azure Data Lake goals?

<--- Score

235. Do you think Azure Data Lake accomplishes the goals you expect it to accomplish?

<--- Score

236. What Azure Data Lake skills are most important?

<--- Score

237. What management system can you use to leverage the Azure Data Lake experience, ideas, and concerns of the people closest to the work to be done?

<--- Score

238. If you were responsible for initiating and implementing major changes in your organization, what steps might you take to ensure acceptance of those changes?

<--- Score

239. What is the estimated value of the project?

<--- Score

240. Can the schedule be done in the given time?
<--- Score

241. Do Azure Data Lake rules make a reasonable demand on a users capabilities?
<--- Score

242. How is social responsibility important in your organizations marketing?
<--- Score

243. Is the order of subdivisions appropriate (placement of geographic subdivision, etc.)?
<--- Score

244. What unique value proposition (UVP) do you offer?
<--- Score

245. Are new benefits received and understood?
<--- Score

246. Which functions and people interact with the supplier and or customer?
<--- Score

247. Are all compliance regulations taken care of?
<--- Score

248. What are the barriers to increased Azure Data Lake production?
<--- Score

249. How do you create buy-in?

<--- Score

250. Are assumptions made in Azure Data Lake stated explicitly?
<--- Score

251. How do customers see your organization?
<--- Score

252. What happens when a new employee joins the organization?
<--- Score

253. How well are you prepared to use it?
<--- Score

254. Why not do Azure Data Lake?
<--- Score

255. Where did it come from?
<--- Score

256. What counts that you are not counting?
<--- Score

257. How will you insure seamless interoperability of Azure Data Lake moving forward?
<--- Score

258. What was the last experiment you ran?
<--- Score

259. How will you motivate the stakeholders with the least vested interest?
<--- Score

260. Can you realistically store everything?
<--- Score

261. What role does communication play in the success or failure of a Azure Data Lake project?
<--- Score

262. How close to the edge can we push the filtering and compression algorithms?
<--- Score

263. If your company went out of business tomorrow, would anyone who doesn't get a paycheck here care?
<--- Score

264. Why should you adopt a Azure Data Lake framework?
<--- Score

265. How will you know that the Azure Data Lake project has been successful?
<--- Score

266. What is the funding source for this project?
<--- Score

267. Nature of the content?
<--- Score

268. If your customer were your grandmother, would you tell her to buy what you're selling?
<--- Score

269. What kind of knowledge does it assess?
<--- Score

270. What are the potential basics of Azure Data Lake fraud?

<--- Score

271. What is tacit permission and approval, anyway?

<--- Score

272. Do you see more potential in people than they do in themselves?

<--- Score

273. How do you transition from the baseline to the target?

<--- Score

274. What tools should be used?

<--- Score

275. Do you have enough freaky customers in your portfolio pushing you to the limit day in and day out?

<--- Score

276. Where are they commonly created?

<--- Score

277. Playing Not to Lose vs. Playing to Win -- were you generally playing defense and have now gone of the offensive?

<--- Score

278. At what moment would you think; Will I get fired?

<--- Score

279. How do you maintain Azure Data Lake's Integrity?

<--- Score

280. Political -is anyone trying to undermine this project?
<--- Score

281. To whom do you add value?
<--- Score

282. How can you become more high-tech but still be high touch?
<--- Score

283. What kinds of use are permitted/prohibited by licenses?
<--- Score

284. Who is responsible for errors?
<--- Score

285. What one word do you want to own in the minds of your customers, employees, and partners?
<--- Score

286. Why should people listen to you?
<--- Score

287. Marketing budgets are tighter, consumers are more skeptical, and social media has changed forever the way we talk about Azure Data Lake. How do you gain traction?
<--- Score

288. What method to use ?
<--- Score

289. What are the components of a subject

authority record?
<--- Score

290. What is your competitive advantage?
<--- Score

291. Who do we want your customers to become?
<--- Score

292. What trophy do you want on your mantle?
<--- Score

293. How do you accomplish your long range Azure Data Lake goals?
<--- Score

294. How would you arrive at the decomposition without such knowledge?
<--- Score

295. What is the source of the strategies for Azure Data Lake strengthening and reform?
<--- Score

296. If this nomination is completed on behalf of the customer, has that customer been made aware of this nomination in advance of this submission?
<--- Score

297. How do you manage the journey?
<--- Score

298. What stupid rule would you most like to kill?
<--- Score

299. Who do you want your customers to become?

<--- Score

300. Will there be any necessary staff changes (redundancies or new hires)?
<--- Score

301. How do you keep the momentum going?
<--- Score

302. Think of your Azure Data Lake project, what are the main functions?
<--- Score

303. Do lakes with different trophic structures differ in resilience?
<--- Score

304. How do you keep records, of what?
<--- Score

305. Do you have past Azure Data Lake successes?
<--- Score

306. What are the nomination criteria?
<--- Score

307. What have been your experiences in defining long range Azure Data Lake goals?
<--- Score

308. How to attract and keep the community involved?
<--- Score

309. How do you set Azure Data Lake stretch targets and how do you get people to not only participate in

setting these stretch targets but also that they strive to achieve these?

<--- Score

310. How ready are you to go there?

<--- Score

311. If you had to rebuild your organization without any traditional competitive advantages (i.e., no killer a technology, promising research, innovative product/ service delivery model, etc.), how would your people have to approach their work and collaborate together in order to create the necessary conditions for success?

<--- Score

312. Does the user interface function as intended?

<--- Score

313. How do you govern and fulfill your societal responsibilities?

<--- Score

314. Are all key stakeholders present at all Structured Walkthroughs?

<--- Score

315. How can you become the company that would put you out of business?

<--- Score

316. From which country is your organisation from?

<--- Score

317. What are the long-term Azure Data Lake goals?

<--- Score

318. Who is collecting what?
<--- Score

319. How do you convince people in your organization who do not work in the marketing department that the customer is the boss?
<--- Score

320. Customer co-creation in service innovation: a matter of communication?
<--- Score

321. What are the rules and assumptions your industry operates under? What if the opposite were true?
<--- Score

322. How do you provide a safe environment -physically and emotionally?
<--- Score

323. How can you incorporate support to ensure safe and effective use of Azure Data Lake into the services that you provide?
<--- Score

324. Is there any reason to believe the opposite of my current belief?
<--- Score

325. What are your most important goals for the strategic Azure Data Lake objectives?
<--- Score

326. What are we collecting?

<--- Score

327. What are the difficulties marketing faces with this approach?
<--- Score

328. Is this technique viable across content areas?
<--- Score

329. How do you go about securing Azure Data Lake?
<--- Score

330. What are the challenges?
<--- Score

331. Did you miss previous insights?
<--- Score

332. What information is critical to your organization that your executives are ignoring?
<--- Score

333. What has been done by your organization to motivate you to work well?
<--- Score

334. Who is the main stakeholder, with ultimate responsibility for driving Azure Data Lake forward?
<--- Score

335. If no one would ever find out about your accomplishments, how would you lead differently?
<--- Score

336. Do you say no to customers for no reason?
<--- Score

337. Who are your customers?
<--- Score

Add up total points for this section:
_ _ _ _ _ = Total points for this section

Divided by: _ _ _ _ _ _ (number of
statements answered) = _ _ _ _ _ _
Average score for this section

Transfer your score to the Azure Data
Lake Index at the beginning of the Self-
Assessment.

Azure Data Lake and Managing Projects, Criteria for Project Managers:

1.0 Initiating Process Group: Azure Data Lake

1. How should needs be met?

2. First of all, should any action be taken?

3. Do you know if the Azure Data Lake project requires outside equipment or vendor resources?

4. What communication items need improvement?

5. How well did the chosen processes fit the needs of the Azure Data Lake project?

6. What are the constraints?

7. Measurable - are the targets measurable?

8. For technology Azure Data Lake projects only: Are all production support stakeholders (Business unit, technical support, & user) prepared for implementation with appropriate contingency plans?

9. Do you know all the stakeholders impacted by the Azure Data Lake project and what needs are?

10. Who is performing the work of the Azure Data Lake project?

11. The Azure Data Lake project managers have maximum authority in which type of organization?

12. What were the challenges that you encountered during the execution of a previous Azure Data Lake

project that you would not want to repeat?

13. Have the stakeholders identified all individual requirements pertaining to business process?

14. The Azure Data Lake project you are managing has nine stakeholders. How many channel of communications are there between corresponding stakeholders?

15. What are the overarching issues of your organization?

16. What must be done?

17. If the risk event occurs, what will you do?

18. Establishment of pm office?

19. Who are the Azure Data Lake project stakeholders?

20. Were resources available as planned?

1.1 Project Charter: Azure Data Lake

21. Why the improvements?

22. What is in it for you?

23. What is the most common tool for helping define the detail?

24. When will this occur?

25. Strategic fit: what is the strategic initiative identifier for this Azure Data Lake project?

26. Why use a Azure Data Lake project charter?

27. Why do you manage integration?

28. Why executive support?

29. Why is it important?

30. How much?

31. What changes can you make to improve?

32. Why do you need to manage scope?

33. If finished, on what date did it finish?

34. Dependent Azure Data Lake projects: what Azure Data Lake projects must be underway or completed before this Azure Data Lake project can be successful?

35. Fit with other Products Compliments – Cannibalizes?

36. Assumptions and constraints: what assumptions were made in defining the Azure Data Lake project?

37. When is a charter needed?

38. Run it as as a startup?

39. Review the general mission What system will be affected by the improvement efforts?

40. Where and how does the team fit within your organization structure?

1.2 Stakeholder Register: Azure Data Lake

41. Who wants to talk about Security?

42. Who is managing stakeholder engagement?

43. How big is the gap?

44. What are the major Azure Data Lake project milestones requiring communications or providing communications opportunities?

45. Who are the stakeholders?

46. How should employers make voices heard?

47. What is the power of the stakeholder?

48. What opportunities exist to provide communications?

49. How much influence do they have on the Azure Data Lake project?

50. What & Why?

51. Is your organization ready for change?

52. How will reports be created?

1.3 Stakeholder Analysis Matrix: Azure Data Lake

53. Timescales, deadlines and pressures?

54. Processes and systems, etc?

55. What resources might the stakeholder bring to the Azure Data Lake project?

56. What unique or lowest-cost resources does the Azure Data Lake project have access to?

57. Guiding question: who shall you involve in the making of the stakeholder map?

58. Why involve the stakeholder?

59. Loss of key staff?

60. Where are the good opportunities facing your organizations development?

61. Management cover, succession?

62. Competitor intentions - various?

63. What do people from other organizations see as your organizations weaknesses?

64. What is your organizations competitors doing?

65. Contributions to policy and practice?

66. Who is most dependent on the resources at stake?

67. Industry or lifestyle trends?

68. Partnerships, agencies, distribution?

69. How affected by the problem(s)?

70. Lack of competitive strength?

71. Resource providers; who can provide resources to ensure the implementation of the Azure Data Lake project?

72. Who will promote/support the Azure Data Lake project, provided that they are involved?

2.0 Planning Process Group: Azure Data Lake

73. When will the Azure Data Lake project be done?

74. Is the identification of the problems, inequalities and gaps, with respective causes, clear in the Azure Data Lake project?

75. How are it Azure Data Lake projects different?

76. How can you tell when you are done?

77. Professionals want to know what is expected from them; what are the deliverables?

78. Azure Data Lake project assessment; why did you do this Azure Data Lake project?

79. If task x starts two days late, what is the effect on the Azure Data Lake project end date?

80. If action is called for, what form should it take?

81. What do they need to know about the Azure Data Lake project?

82. Do the partners have sufficient financial capacity to keep up the benefits produced by the programme?

83. If a risk event occurs, what will you do?

84. Did you read it correctly?

85. What factors are contributing to progress or delay in the achievement of products and results?

86. How will users learn how to use the deliverables?

87. What is the difference between the early schedule and late schedule?

88. Who are the Azure Data Lake project stakeholders?

89. To what extent do the intervention objectives and strategies of the Azure Data Lake project respond to your organizations plans?

90. What are the different approaches to building the WBS?

91. How well defined and documented are the Azure Data Lake project management processes you chose to use?

92. Are the necessary foundations in place to ensure the sustainability of the results of the Azure Data Lake project?

2.1 Project Management Plan: Azure Data Lake

93. Do the proposed changes from the Azure Data Lake project include any significant risks to safety?

94. Are comparable cost estimates used for comparing, screening and selecting alternative plans, and has a reasonable cost estimate been developed for the recommended plan?

95. Are cost risk analysis methods applied to develop contingencies for the estimated total Azure Data Lake project costs?

96. Was the peer (technical) review of the cost estimates duly coordinated with the cost estimate center of expertise and addressed in the review documentation and certification?

97. Is the budget realistic?

98. Is there anything you would now do differently on your Azure Data Lake project based on past experience?

99. What are the training needs?

100. What would you do differently?

101. How can you best help your organization to develop consistent practices in Azure Data Lake project management planning stages?

102. Are calculations and results of analyzes essentially correct?

103. Does the selected plan protect privacy?

104. How well are you able to manage your risk?

105. What would you do differently what did not work?

106. How do you manage integration?

107. What does management expect of PMs?

108. If the Azure Data Lake project is complex or scope is specialized, do you have appropriate and/or qualified staff available to perform the tasks?

109. What are the deliverables?

110. Are the proposed Azure Data Lake project purposes different than a previously authorized Azure Data Lake project?

111. Did the planning effort collaborate to develop solutions that integrate expertise, policies, programs, and Azure Data Lake projects across entities?

112. Does the implementation plan have an appropriate division of responsibilities?

2.2 Scope Management Plan: Azure Data Lake

113. Is there a requirements change management processes in place?

114. Deliverables -are the deliverables tangible and verifiable?

115. Is mitigation authorized or recommended?

116. Are metrics used to evaluate and manage Vendors?

117. Would the Azure Data Lake project cost sharing involve reimbursement to the sponsor?

118. Has a capability assessment been conducted?

119. Are adequate resources provided for the quality assurance function?

120. Is your organization structure for both tracking & controlling the budget well defined and assigned to a specific individual?

121. Does all Azure Data Lake project documentation reside in a common repository for easy access?

122. How difficult will it be to do specific activities on this Azure Data Lake project?

123. Are the proposed Azure Data Lake project

purposes different than the previously authorized Azure Data Lake project?

124. Pop quiz – which are the same inputs as in scope planning?

125. How do you plan to control Scope Creep?

126. Has allowance been made for vacations, holidays, training (learning time for each team member), staff promotions & staff turnovers?

127. Has the schedule been baselined?

128. What are the risks that could significantly affect the budget of the Azure Data Lake project?

129. Was the scope definition used in task sequencing?

130. Without-plan conditions?

131. Has your organization readiness assessment been conducted?

2.3 Requirements Management Plan: Azure Data Lake

132. Does the Azure Data Lake project have a Change Control process?

133. Who will approve the requirements (and if multiple approvers, in what order)?

134. How will bidders price evaluations be done, by deliverables, phases, or in a big bang?

135. Did you avoid subjective, flowery or non-specific statements?

136. Is requirements work dependent on any other specific Azure Data Lake project or non-Azure Data Lake project activities (e.g. funding, approvals, procurement)?

137. Which hardware or software, related to, or as outcome of the Azure Data Lake project is new to your organization?

138. How often will the reporting occur?

139. The wbs is developed as part of a joint planning session. and how do you know that youhave done this right?

140. Who will do the reporting and to whom will reports be delivered?

141. Should you include sub-activities?

142. How detailed should the Azure Data Lake project get?

143. Controlling Azure Data Lake project requirements involves monitoring the status of the Azure Data Lake project requirements and managing changes to the requirements. Who is responsible for monitoring and tracking the Azure Data Lake project requirements?

144. Will the Azure Data Lake project requirements become approved in writing?

145. Will the contractors involved take full responsibility?

146. Who is responsible for monitoring and tracking the Azure Data Lake project requirements?

147. How will requirements be managed?

148. Could inaccurate or incomplete requirements in this Azure Data Lake project create a serious risk for the business?

149. Is infrastructure setup part of your Azure Data Lake project?

150. Are actual resource expenditures versus planned still acceptable?

151. After the requirements are gathered and set forth on the requirements register, theyre little more than a laundry list of items. Some may be duplicates,

some might conflict with others and some will be too broad or too vague to understand. Describe how the requirements will be analyzed. Who will perform the analysis?

2.4 Requirements Documentation: Azure Data Lake

152. What kind of entity is a problem ?

153. Do your constraints stand?

154. What are current process problems?

155. Is the requirement realistically testable?

156. What variations exist for a process?

157. How much testing do you need to do to prove that your system is safe?

158. Who provides requirements?

159. Have the benefits identified with the system being identified clearly?

160. What is a show stopper in the requirements?

161. Are there legal issues?

162. Do technical resources exist?

163. What happens when requirements are wrong?

164. How do you get the user to tell you what they want?

165. What are the attributes of a customer?

166. Who is interacting with the system?

167. What can tools do for us?

168. Completeness. are all functions required by the customer included?

169. How much does requirements engineering cost?

170. What if the system wasn t implemented?

171. What images does it conjure?

2.5 Requirements Traceability Matrix: Azure Data Lake

172. How do you manage scope?

173. How small is small enough?

174. Will you use a Requirements Traceability Matrix?

175. Describe the process for approving requirements so they can be added to the traceability matrix and Azure Data Lake project work can be performed. Will the Azure Data Lake project requirements become approved in writing?

176. What is the WBS?

177. What are the chronologies, contingencies, consequences, criteria?

178. Why do you manage scope?

179. How will it affect the stakeholders personally in their career?

180. Why use a WBS?

181. Do you have a clear understanding of all subcontracts in place?

182. Is there a requirements traceability process in place?

183. What percentage of Azure Data Lake projects are producing traceability matrices between requirements and other work products?

2.6 Project Scope Statement: Azure Data Lake

184. Elements of scope management that deal with concept development ?

185. Are the meetings set up to have assigned note takers that will add action/issues to the issue list?

186. Were key Azure Data Lake project stakeholders brought into the Azure Data Lake project Plan?

187. Did your Azure Data Lake project ask for this?

188. Once its defined, what is the stability of the Azure Data Lake project scope?

189. Elements that deal with providing the detail?

190. Are there adequate Azure Data Lake project control systems?

191. What are the defined meeting materials?

192. What went right?

193. Is there an information system for the Azure Data Lake project?

194. Risks?

195. Azure Data Lake project lead, team lead, solution architect?

196. Identify how your team and you will create the Azure Data Lake project scope statement and the work breakdown structure (WBS). Document how you will create the Azure Data Lake project scope statement and WBS, and make sure you answer the following questions: In defining Azure Data Lake project scope and the WBS, will you and your Azure Data Lake project team be using methods defined by your organization, methods defined by the Azure Data Lake project management office (PMO), or other methods?

197. Is there a Change Management Board?

198. Is the Azure Data Lake project manager qualified and experienced in Azure Data Lake project management?

199. Will the risk documents be filed?

200. Is your organization structure appropriate for the Azure Data Lake projects size and complexity?

201. Will you need a statement of work?

202. How will you haverify the accuracy of the work of the Azure Data Lake project, and what constitutes acceptance of the deliverables?

203. Do you anticipate new stakeholders joining the Azure Data Lake project over time?

2.7 Assumption and Constraint Log: Azure Data Lake

204. Is the definition of the Azure Data Lake project scope clear; what needs to be accomplished?

205. Do the requirements meet the standards of correctness, completeness, consistency, accuracy, and readability?

206. Are formal code reviews conducted?

207. Are there ways to reduce the time it takes to get something approved?

208. How do you design an auditing system?

209. What worked well?

210. What if failure during recovery?

211. What do you log?

212. Are there processes in place to ensure internal consistency between the source code components?

213. How many Azure Data Lake project staff does this specific process affect?

214. What to do at recovery?

215. Would known impacts serve as impediments?

216. Are requirements management tracking tools and procedures in place?

217. How relevant is this attribute to this Azure Data Lake project or audit?

218. What threats might prevent you from getting there?

219. How can constraints be violated?

220. Does a documented Azure Data Lake project organizational policy & plan (i.e. governance model) exist?

221. If it is out of compliance, should the process be amended or should the Plan be amended?

222. Have all necessary approvals been obtained?

223. What do you audit?

2.8 Work Breakdown Structure: Azure Data Lake

224. How far down?

225. Is it a change in scope?

226. Why would you develop a Work Breakdown Structure?

227. Do you need another level?

228. Who has to do it?

229. How big is a work-package?

230. Why is it useful?

231. Is the work breakdown structure (wbs) defined and is the scope of the Azure Data Lake project clear with assigned deliverable owners?

232. How much detail?

233. What is the probability that the Azure Data Lake project duration will exceed xx weeks?

234. When does it have to be done?

235. Is it still viable?

236. When do you stop?

237. How will you and your Azure Data Lake project team define the Azure Data Lake projects scope and work breakdown structure?

238. When would you develop a Work Breakdown Structure?

239. What has to be done?

240. Can you make it?

241. How many levels?

242. Where does it take place?

243. What is the probability of completing the Azure Data Lake project in less that xx days?

2.9 WBS Dictionary: Azure Data Lake

244. Are data elements summarized through the functional organizational structure for progressively higher levels of management?

245. Authorization to proceed with all authorized work?

246. Does the contractors system include procedures for measuring the performance of critical subcontractors?

247. Does the contractors system provide for determination of price variance by comparing planned Vs actual commitments?

248. Are all authorized tasks assigned to identified organizational elements?

249. Are estimates developed by Azure Data Lake project personnel coordinated with the already stated responsible for overall management to determine whether required resources will be available according to revised planning?

250. Are work packages assigned to performing organizations?

251. Does the contractor have procedures which permit identification of recurring or non-recurring costs as necessary?

252. Does the contractors system provide for accurate

cost accumulation and assignment to control accounts in a manner consistent with the budgets using recognized acceptable costing techniques?

253. Changes in the direct base to which overhead costs are allocated?

254. Budgets assigned to major functional organizations?

255. Evaluate the performance of operating organizations?

256. Are the requirements for all items of overhead established by rational, traceable processes?

257. Are procedures in existence that control replanning of unopened work packages, and are corresponding procedures adhered to?

258. Is the work done on a work package level as described in the WBS dictionary?

259. Changes in the nature of the overhead requirements?

260. What is the goal?

2.10 Schedule Management Plan: Azure Data Lake

261. Is there an excessive and invalid use of task constraints and relationships of leads/lags?

262. Are Azure Data Lake project leaders committed to this Azure Data Lake project full time?

263. Is there a formal set of procedures supporting Issues Management?

264. Is an industry recognized mechanized support tool(s) being used for Azure Data Lake project scheduling & tracking?

265. Is there a procedure for management, control and release of schedule margin?

266. Can additional resources be added to subsequent tasks to reduce the durations of the already stated tasks?

267. Have stakeholder accountabilities & responsibilities been clearly defined?

268. Are right task and resource calendars used in the IMS?

269. Can be realistically shortened (the duration of subsequent tasks)?

270. Is funded schedule margin reasonable and

logically distributed?

271. Are scheduled deliverables actually delivered?

272. Are the people assigned to the Azure Data Lake project sufficiently qualified?

273. Time for overtime?

274. Are assumptions being identified, recorded, analyzed, qualified and closed?

275. Does the time Azure Data Lake projection include an amount for contingencies (time reserves)?

276. Have all involved Azure Data Lake project stakeholders and work groups committed to the Azure Data Lake project?

277. Are procurement deliverables arriving on time and to specification?

278. Are schedule performance measures defined including pre-set triggers for specific actions?

2.11 Activity List: Azure Data Lake

279. What is your organizations history in doing similar activities?

280. What is the total time required to complete the Azure Data Lake project if no delays occur?

281. Can you determine the activity that must finish, before this activity can start?

282. Is infrastructure setup part of your Azure Data Lake project?

283. How much slack is available in the Azure Data Lake project?

284. Is there anything planned that does not need to be here?

285. When do the individual activities need to start and finish?

286. What went wrong?

287. What are you counting on?

288. How difficult will it be to do specific activities on this Azure Data Lake project?

289. How do you determine the late start (LS) for each activity?

290. What will be performed?

291. Who will perform the work?

292. What is the probability the Azure Data Lake project can be completed in xx weeks?

293. How can the Azure Data Lake project be displayed graphically to better visualize the activities?

294. How detailed should a Azure Data Lake project get?

295. For other activities, how much delay can be tolerated?

296. How will it be performed?

297. What is the LF and LS for each activity?

2.12 Activity Attributes: Azure Data Lake

298. How much activity detail is required?

299. Is there a trend during the year?

300. Resources to accomplish the work?

301. Which method produces the more accurate cost assignment?

302. Were there other ways you could have organized the data to achieve similar results?

303. Resource is assigned to?

304. How do you manage time?

305. Activity: fair or not fair?

306. How else could the items be grouped?

307. How difficult will it be to do specific activities on this Azure Data Lake project?

308. Would you consider either of corresponding activities an outlier?

309. Does your organization of the data change its meaning?

310. Why?

311. What is the general pattern here?

312. Can you re-assign any activities to another resource to resolve an over-allocation?

313. Are the required resources available or need to be acquired?

314. Have you identified the Activity Leveling Priority code value on each activity?

315. Are the required resources available?

2.13 Milestone List: Azure Data Lake

316. Milestone pages should display the UserID of the person who added the milestone. Does a report or query exist that provides this audit information?

317. What date will the task finish?

318. What has been done so far?

319. Competitive advantages?

320. Reliability of data, plan predictability?

321. Can you derive how soon can the whole Azure Data Lake project finish?

322. Do you foresee any technical risks or developmental challenges?

323. How difficult will it be to do specific activities on this Azure Data Lake project?

324. How will you get the word out to customers?

325. Usps (unique selling points)?

326. Describe the concept of the technology, product or service that will be or has been developed. How will it be used?

327. How late can each activity be finished and started?

328. Information and research?

329. Sustainable financial backing?

330. Obstacles faced?

331. Global influences?

2.14 Network Diagram: Azure Data Lake

332. What can be done concurrently?

333. Are you on time?

334. Which type of network diagram allows you to depict four types of dependencies?

335. What activities must follow this activity?

336. Will crashing x weeks return more in benefits than it costs?

337. What is the completion time?

338. If x is long, what would be the completion time if you break x into two parallel parts of y weeks and z weeks?

339. Are the gantt chart and/or network diagram updated periodically and used to assess the overall Azure Data Lake project timetable?

340. Where do you schedule uncertainty time?

341. What must be completed before an activity can be started?

342. Can you calculate the confidence level?

343. What are the Key Success Factors?

344. What are the Major Administrative Issues?

345. What are the tools?

346. Exercise: what is the probability that the Azure Data Lake project duration will exceed xx weeks?

347. What activities must occur simultaneously with this activity?

348. If the Azure Data Lake project network diagram cannot change and you have extra personnel resources, what is the BEST thing to do?

349. How difficult will it be to do specific activities on this Azure Data Lake project?

2.15 Activity Resource Requirements: Azure Data Lake

350. How do you handle petty cash?

351. Are there unresolved issues that need to be addressed?

352. Do you use tools like decomposition and rolling-wave planning to produce the activity list and other outputs?

353. What is the Work Plan Standard?

354. How many signatures do you require on a check and does this match what is in your policy and procedures?

355. Anything else?

356. Other support in specific areas?

357. When does monitoring begin?

358. Why do you do that?

359. Organizational Applicability?

360. What are constraints that you might find during the Human Resource Planning process?

361. Which logical relationship does the PDM use most often?

2.16 Resource Breakdown Structure: Azure Data Lake

362. What is the difference between % Complete and % work?

363. When do they need the information?

364. Who is allowed to see what data about which resources?

365. What is each stakeholders desired outcome for the Azure Data Lake project?

366. What defines a successful Azure Data Lake project?

367. Any changes from stakeholders?

368. What is the purpose of assigning and documenting responsibility?

369. How should the information be delivered?

370. What is the primary purpose of the human resource plan?

371. Who delivers the information?

372. Why is this important?

373. Who is allowed to perform which functions?

374. Changes based on input from stakeholders?

375. Why do you do it?

376. Which resource planning tool provides information on resource responsibility and accountability?

377. Who will use the system?

2.17 Activity Duration Estimates: Azure Data Lake

378. Explanation notice how many choices are half right?

379. (Cpi), and schedule performance index (spi) for the Azure Data Lake project?

380. After how many days will the lease cost be the same as the purchase cost for the equipment?

381. How does Azure Data Lake project integration management relate to the Azure Data Lake project life cycle, stakeholders, and the other Azure Data Lake project management knowledge areas?

382. How much time is required to develop it?

383. How do functionality, system outputs, performance, reliability, and maintainability requirements affect quality planning?

384. Are operational definitions created to identify quality measurement criteria for specific activities?

385. What is earned value?

386. Which skills do you think are most important for an information technology Azure Data Lake project manager?

387. Do scope statements include the Azure Data

Lake project objectives and expected deliverables?

388. Is a contract change control system defined to manage changes to contract terms and conditions?

389. If the optimiztic estimate for an activity is 12days, and the pessimistic estimate is 18days, what is the standard deviation of this activity?

390. Does a process exist to identify Azure Data Lake project roles, responsibilities and reporting relationships?

391. What type of information goes in a quality assurance plan?

392. Do you agree with the suggestions provided for improving Azure Data Lake project communications?

393. What type of people would you want on your team?

394. On which process should team members spend the most time?

2.18 Duration Estimating Worksheet: Azure Data Lake

395. What is your role?

396. Do any colleagues have experience with your organization and/or RFPs?

397. What is an Average Azure Data Lake project?

398. Does the Azure Data Lake project provide innovative ways for stakeholders to overcome obstacles or deliver better outcomes?

399. Done before proceeding with this activity or what can be done concurrently?

400. When, then?

401. Will the Azure Data Lake project collaborate with the local community and leverage resources?

402. Why estimate costs?

403. What questions do you have?

404. What utility impacts are there?

405. Small or large Azure Data Lake project?

406. What are the critical bottleneck activities?

407. Define the work as completely as possible. What

work will be included in the Azure Data Lake project?

408. When does your organization expect to be able to complete it?

409. What is cost and Azure Data Lake project cost management?

410. Is the Azure Data Lake project responsive to community need?

411. How can the Azure Data Lake project be displayed graphically to better visualize the activities?

412. What info is needed?

2.19 Project Schedule: Azure Data Lake

413. How do you know that youhave done this right?

414. Was the Azure Data Lake project schedule reviewed by all stakeholders and formally accepted?

415. Activity charts and bar charts are graphical representations of a Azure Data Lake project schedule ...how do they differ?

416. How do you manage Azure Data Lake project Risk?

417. Are activities connected because logic dictates the order in which others occur?

418. Month Azure Data Lake project take?

419. Is there a Schedule Management Plan that establishes the criteria and activities for developing, monitoring and controlling the Azure Data Lake project schedule?

420. Is infrastructure setup part of your Azure Data Lake project?

421. Why or why not?

422. Is Azure Data Lake project work proceeding in accordance with the original Azure Data Lake project schedule?

423. How closely did the initial Azure Data Lake project Schedule compare with the actual schedule?

424. Are quality inspections and review activities listed in the Azure Data Lake project schedule(s)?

425. What is the most mis-scheduled part of process?

426. If there are any qualifying green components to this Azure Data Lake project, what portion of the total Azure Data Lake project cost is green?

427. How effectively were issues able to be resolved without impacting the Azure Data Lake project Schedule or Budget?

428. How do you use schedules?

429. What is risk?

2.20 Cost Management Plan: Azure Data Lake

430. Are software metrics formally captured, analyzed and used as a basis for other Azure Data Lake project estimates?

431. What is an Acceptance Management Process?

432. Schedule contingency – how will the schedule contingency be administrated?

433. Is the assigned Azure Data Lake project manager a PMP (Certified Azure Data Lake project manager) and experienced?

434. What weaknesses do you have?

435. Environmental management – what changes in statutory environmental compliance requirements are anticipated during the Azure Data Lake project?

436. Will the earned value reporting interface between time and cost management?

437. Will the forecasts be based on trend analysis and earned value statistics?

438. Is your organization certified as a supplier, wholesaler and/or regular dealer?

439. Do Azure Data Lake project managers participating in the Azure Data Lake project know the

Azure Data Lake projects true status first hand?

440. Has the budget been baselined?

441. Is there an on-going process in place to monitor Azure Data Lake project risks?

442. Are change requests logged and managed?

443. Azure Data Lake project Objectives?

444. Are meeting objectives identified for each meeting?

445. For cost control purposes?

446. Was the Azure Data Lake project schedule reviewed by all stakeholders and formally accepted?

447. Have the key functions and capabilities been defined and assigned to each release or iteration?

448. Quality assurance overheads?

2.21 Activity Cost Estimates: Azure Data Lake

449. Review – what are some common errors in activities to avoid?

450. Based on your Azure Data Lake project communication management plan, what worked well?

451. Performance bond should always provide what part of the contract value?

452. Scope statement only direct or indirect costs as well?

453. What is a Azure Data Lake project Management Plan?

454. What is Azure Data Lake project cost management?

455. Were decisions made in a timely manner?

456. How do you fund change orders?

457. Where can you get activity reports?

458. Are data needed on characteristics of care?

459. Eac -estimate at completion, what is the total job expected to cost?

460. One way to define activities is to consider how organization employees describe jobs to families and friends. You basically want to know, What do you do?

461. Vac -variance at completion, how much over/ under budget do you expect to be?

462. How do you treat administrative costs in the activity inventory?

463. In which phase of the acquisition process cycle does source qualifications reside?

464. Was it performed on time?

465. How difficult will it be to do specific tasks on the Azure Data Lake project?

466. What makes a good activity description?

467. Were sponsors and decision makers available when needed outside regularly scheduled meetings?

468. Can you change your activities?

2.22 Cost Estimating Worksheet: Azure Data Lake

469. What happens to any remaining funds not used?

470. Does the Azure Data Lake project provide innovative ways for stakeholders to overcome obstacles or deliver better outcomes?

471. What will others want?

472. What additional Azure Data Lake project(s) could be initiated as a result of this Azure Data Lake project?

473. How will the results be shared and to whom?

474. Who is best positioned to know and assist in identifying corresponding factors?

475. What can be included?

476. Will the Azure Data Lake project collaborate with the local community and leverage resources?

477. Is the Azure Data Lake project responsive to community need?

478. What costs are to be estimated?

479. Is it feasible to establish a control group arrangement?

480. Identify the timeframe necessary to monitor

progress and collect data to determine how the selected measure has changed?

481. What is the purpose of estimating?

482. What is the estimated labor cost today based upon this information?

483. Value pocket identification & quantification what are value pockets?

484. Ask: are others positioned to know, are others credible, and will others cooperate?

485. Can a trend be established from historical performance data on the selected measure and are the criteria for using trend analysis or forecasting methods met?

2.23 Cost Baseline: Azure Data Lake

486. Are procedures defined by which the cost baseline may be changed?

487. If you sold 10x widgets on a day, what would the affect on profits be?

488. What do you want to measure ?

489. Does the suggested change request represent a desired enhancement to the products functionality?

490. Azure Data Lake project goals -should others be reconsidered?

491. How accurate do cost estimates need to be?

492. Is request in line with priorities?

493. Are there contingencies or conditions related to the acceptance?

494. Has the Azure Data Lake projected annual cost to operate and maintain the product(s) or service(s) been approved and funded?

495. How do you manage cost?

496. Will the Azure Data Lake project fail if the change request is not executed?

497. Is there anything unique in this Azure Data Lake projects scope statement that will affect resources?

498. Have the resources used by the Azure Data Lake project been reassigned to other units or Azure Data Lake projects?

499. Has the Azure Data Lake project documentation been archived or otherwise disposed as described in the Azure Data Lake project communication plan?

500. Have all approved changes to the Azure Data Lake project requirement been identified and impact on the performance, cost, and schedule baselines documented?

501. What is your organizations history in doing similar tasks?

502. What would the life cycle costs be?

2.24 Quality Management Plan: Azure Data Lake

503. Does the Azure Data Lake project have a formal Azure Data Lake project Plan?

504. Checking the completeness and appropriateness of the sampling and testing. Were the right locations/ samples tested for the right parameters?

505. How do senior leaders review organizational performance?

506. How are calibration records kept?

507. How does your organization measure customer satisfaction/dissatisfaction?

508. Is there a Steering Committee in place?

509. Methodology followed?

510. Do you periodically review your data quality system to see that it is up to date and appropriate?

511. How does your organization perform analyzes to assess overall organizational performance and set priorities?

512. Have adequate resources been provided by management to ensure Azure Data Lake project success?

513. How are changes to procedures made?

514. How are deviations from procedures handled?

515. What does it do for you (or to me)?

516. How is staff informed of proper reporting methods?

517. Does the system design reflect the requirements?

518. How does your organization make it easy for customers to seek assistance or complain?

519. What field records are generated?

520. Show/provide copy of procedures for taking field notes?

521. Have Azure Data Lake project management standards and procedures been established and documented?

522. How do senior leaders create your organizational focus on customers and other stakeholders?

2.25 Quality Metrics: Azure Data Lake

523. What approved evidence based screening tools can be used?

524. Do you know how much profit a 10% decrease in waste would generate?

525. Were number of defects identified?

526. Where did complaints, returns and warranty claims come from?

527. Which data do others need in one place to target areas of improvement?

528. Is a risk containment plan in place?

529. Product Availability ?

530. What documentation is required?

531. Subjective quality component: customer satisfaction, how do you measure it?

532. What can manufacturing professionals do to ensure quality is seen as an integral part of the entire product lifecycle?

533. Is there a set of procedures to capture, analyze and act on quality metrics?

534. How are requirements conflicts resolved?

535. The metrics–what is being considered?

536. How should customers provide input?

537. Are applicable standards referenced and available?

538. Who notifies stakeholders of normal and abnormal results?

539. Is the reporting frequency appropriate?

540. Which are the right metrics to use?

541. Have alternatives been defined in the event that failure occurs?

542. What happens if you get an abnormal result?

2.26 Process Improvement Plan: Azure Data Lake

543. Have the supporting tools been developed or acquired?

544. Why quality management?

545. What lessons have you learned so far?

546. What personnel are the champions for the initiative?

547. Who should prepare the process improvement action plan?

548. The motive is determined by asking, Why do you want to achieve this goal?

549. Everyone agrees on what process improvement is, right?

550. If a process improvement framework is being used, which elements will help the problems and goals listed?

551. How do you measure?

552. Have the frequency of collection and the points in the process where measurements will be made been determined?

553. Does explicit definition of the measures exist?

554. Where do you want to be?

555. Why do you want to achieve the goal?

556. Does your process ensure quality?

557. Management commitment at all levels?

558. Are there forms and procedures to collect and record the data?

559. Where are you now?

560. What is the test-cycle concept?

561. To elicit goal statements, do you ask a question such as, What do you want to achieve?

562. Are you making progress on the improvement framework?

2.27 Responsibility Assignment Matrix: Azure Data Lake

563. Too many is: do all the identified roles need to be routinely informed or only in exceptional circumstances?

564. Do all the identified groups or people really need to be consulted?

565. Identify potential or actual overruns and underruns?

566. Is budgeted cost for work performed calculated in a manner consistent with the way work is planned?

567. What do people write/say on status/Azure Data Lake project reports?

568. Who is responsible for work and budgets for each wbs?

569. With too many people labeled as doing the work, are there too many hands involved?

570. Competencies and craftsmanship – what competencies are necessary and what level?

571. Wbs elements contractually specified for reporting of status (lowest level only)?

572. How do you assist them to be as productive as possible?

573. The total budget for the contract (including estimates for authorized and unpriced work)?

574. Too many rs: with too many people labeled as doing the work, are there too many hands involved?

575. Do you know how your people are allocated?

576. Are material costs reported within the same period as that in which BCWP is earned for that material?

577. Will too many Signing-off responsibilities delay the completion of the activity/deliverable?

578. Do work packages consist of discrete tasks which are adequately described?

2.28 Roles and Responsibilities: Azure Data Lake

579. What is working well?

580. Key conclusions and recommendations: Are conclusions and recommendations relevant and acceptable?

581. What areas would you highlight for changes or improvements?

582. What specific behaviors did you observe?

583. What are your major roles and responsibilities in the area of performance measurement and assessment?

584. What should you do now to ensure that you are meeting all expectations of your current position?

585. Where are you most strong as a supervisor?

586. Are governance roles and responsibilities documented?

587. What areas of supervision are challenging for you?

588. Attainable / achievable: the goal is attainable; can you actually accomplish the goal?

589. Was the expectation clearly communicated?

590. What should you do now to prepare for your career 5+ years from now?

591. Implementation of actions: Who are the responsible units?

592. Have you ever been a part of this team?

593. Is there a training program in place for stakeholders covering expectations, roles and responsibilities and any addition knowledge others need to be good stakeholders?

594. Who is responsible for implementation activities and where will the functions, roles and responsibilities be defined?

595. Is feedback clearly communicated and non-judgmental?

596. Accountabilities: what are the roles and responsibilities of individual team members?

597. Influence: what areas of organizational decision making are you able to influence when you do not have authority to make the final decision?

2.29 Human Resource Management Plan: Azure Data Lake

598. Are the quality tools and methods identified in the Quality Plan appropriate to the Azure Data Lake project?

599. Are staff skills known and available for each task?

600. Are the results of quality assurance reviews provided to affected groups & individuals?

601. Have all unresolved risks been documented?

602. Have Azure Data Lake project success criteria been defined?

603. What commitments have been made?

604. Have adequate resources been provided by management to ensure Azure Data Lake project success?

605. Cost / benefit analysis?

606. How do you determine what key skills and talents are needed to meet the objectives. Is your organization primarily focused on a specific industry?

607. Who is involved?

608. Are action items captured and managed?

609. Do people have the competencies to meet the strategic objectives?

610. Are post milestone Azure Data Lake project reviews (PMPR) conducted with your organization at least once a year?

611. Are the right people being attracted and retained to meet the future challenges?

612. Has the business need been clearly defined?

613. Quality of people required to meet the forecast needs of the department?

614. Have process improvement efforts been completed before requirements efforts begin?

615. Have Azure Data Lake project team accountabilities & responsibilities been clearly defined?

616. Is there a formal process for updating the Azure Data Lake project baseline?

2.30 Communications Management Plan: Azure Data Lake

617. Do you feel a register helps?

618. Are stakeholders internal or external?

619. Are others needed?

620. Do you prepare stakeholder engagement plans?

621. Who is the stakeholder?

622. What data is going to be required?

623. Why is stakeholder engagement important?

624. Which stakeholders are thought leaders, influences, or early adopters?

625. Where do team members get information?

626. How were corresponding initiatives successful?

627. How often do you engage with stakeholders?

628. Do you have members of your team responsible for certain stakeholders?

629. How did the term stakeholder originate?

630. Timing: when do the effects of the communication take place?

631. Are there too many who have an interest in some aspect of your work?

632. What is the political influence?

633. What are the interrelationships?

634. In your work, how much time is spent on stakeholder identification?

635. Who to share with?

636. Can you think of other people who might have concerns or interests?

2.31 Risk Management Plan: Azure Data Lake

637. Have customers been involved fully in the definition of requirements?

638. Have you worked with the customer in the past?

639. Can you stabilize dynamic risk factors?

640. Anticipated volatility of the requirements?

641. Do you train all developers in the process?

642. Market risk -will the new service or product be useful to your organization or marketable to others?

643. Which is an input to the risk management process?

644. Technology risk: is the Azure Data Lake project technically feasible?

645. Do you manage the process through use of metrics?

646. Does the Azure Data Lake project team have experience with the technology to be implemented?

647. Are you working on the right risks?

648. Methodology: how will risk management be performed on this Azure Data Lake project?

649. Maximize short-term return on investment?

650. Are team members trained in the use of the tools?

651. How is risk response planning performed?

652. How well were you able to manage your risk before?

653. What is the likelihood?

654. How would you suggest monitoring for risk transition indicators?

655. What did not work so well?

656. Who should be notified of the occurrence of each of the indicators?

2.32 Risk Register: Azure Data Lake

657. How are risks graded?

658. What is a Community Risk Register?

659. What are the main aims, objectives of the policy, strategy, or service and the intended outcomes?

660. Are implemented controls working as others should?

661. What could prevent you delivering on the strategic program objectives and what is being done to mitigate corresponding issues?

662. Assume the event happens, what is the Most Likely impact?

663. What has changed since the last period?

664. Are corrective measures implemented as planned?

665. Preventative actions - planned actions to reduce the likelihood a risk will occur and/or reduce the seriousness should it occur. What should you do now?

666. Technology risk -is the Azure Data Lake project technically feasible?

667. What should you do now?

668. What is the probability and impact of the risk

occurring?

669. What are you going to do to limit the Azure Data Lake projects risk exposure due to the identified risks?

670. What is the reason for current performance gaps and do the risks and opportunities identified previously account for this?

671. Contingency actions - planned actions to reduce the immediate seriousness of the risk when it does occur. What should you do when?

672. Do you require further engagement?

673. Risk categories: what are the main categories of risks that should be addressed on this Azure Data Lake project?

2.33 Probability and Impact Assessment: Azure Data Lake

674. Is there additional information that would make you more confident about your analysis?

675. What are the current demands of the customer?

676. Assumptions analysis -what assumptions have you made or been given about your Azure Data Lake project?

677. Are tools for analysis and design available?

678. How realistic is the timing of introduction?

679. What things might go wrong?

680. Is the process supported by tools?

681. Is the present organizational structure for handling the Azure Data Lake project sufficient?

682. Risk urgency assessment -which of your risks could occur soon, or require a longer planning time?

683. What should be the external organizations responsibility vis-à-vis total stake in the Azure Data Lake project?

684. Can the risk be avoided by choosing a different alternative?

685. What are the current or emerging trends of culture?

686. What will be the likely political situation during the life of the Azure Data Lake project?

687. Assuming that you have identified a number of risks in the Azure Data Lake project, how would you prioritize them?

688. Are the risk data timely and relevant?

689. Is the delay in one subAzure Data Lake project going to affect another?

690. Are testing tools available and suitable?

691. Are the facilities, expertise, resources, and management know-how available to handle the situation?

692. Is the customer willing to participate in reviews?

2.34 Probability and Impact Matrix: Azure Data Lake

693. Brain storm – mind maps, what if?

694. How will economic events and trends likely affect the Azure Data Lake project?

695. Is the technology to be built new to your organization?

696. Who is going to be the consortium leader?

697. What is Azure Data Lake project risk management?

698. Which of the risk factors can be avoided altogether?

699. Have you ascribed a level of confidence to every critical technical objective?

700. Which risks need to move on to Perform Quantitative Risk Analysis?

701. What would be the effect of slippage?

702. What will be cost of redeployment of the personnel?

703. Pay attention to the quality of the plans: is the content complete, or does it seem to be lacking detail?

704. Is the Azure Data Lake project cutting across the entire organization?

705. Does the customer have a solid idea of what is required?

706. What is the likelihood of a breakthrough?

707. Which should be probably done NEXT?

708. Lay ground work for future returns?

709. What risks were tracked?

710. Are the best people available?

711. How completely has the customer been identified?

2.35 Risk Data Sheet: Azure Data Lake

712. What is the duration of infection (the length of time the host is infected with the organizm) in a normal healthy human host?

713. What is the chance that it will happen?

714. Do effective diagnostic tests exist?

715. What can happen?

716. What were the Causes that contributed?

717. What actions can be taken to eliminate or remove risk?

718. Has the most cost-effective solution been chosen?

719. Risk of what?

720. Is the data sufficiently specified in terms of the type of failure being analyzed, and its frequency or probability?

721. What if client refuses?

722. Type of risk identified?

723. How reliable is the data source?

724. What do you know?

725. What was measured?

726. During work activities could hazards exist?

727. Who has a vested interest in how you perform as your organization (our stakeholders)?

728. What is the likelihood of it happening?

729. What can you do?

730. How do you handle product safely?

731. Has a sensitivity analysis been carried out?

2.36 Procurement Management Plan: Azure Data Lake

732. Have the procedures for identifying budget variances been followed?

733. Is there general agreement & acceptance of the current status and progress of the Azure Data Lake project?

734. If independent estimates will be needed as evaluation criteria, who will prepare them and when?

735. Are parking lot items captured?

736. Are target dates established for each milestone deliverable?

737. Is a payment system in place with proper reviews and approvals?

738. Is the current scope of the Azure Data Lake project substantially different than that originally defined?

739. Is Azure Data Lake project status reviewed with the steering and executive teams at appropriate intervals?

740. Are the Azure Data Lake project plans updated on a frequent basis?

741. Staffing Requirements?

742. Are the payment terms being followed?

743. Are Azure Data Lake project leaders committed to this Azure Data Lake project full time?

744. Has a structured approach been used to break work effort into manageable components (WBS)?

745. Does the detailed work plan match the complexity of tasks with the capabilities of personnel?

746. Are tasks tracked by hours?

747. Is the steering committee active in Azure Data Lake project oversight?

748. Are all resource assumptions documented?

2.37 Source Selection Criteria: Azure Data Lake

749. Can you reasonably estimate total organization requirements for the coming year?

750. What evidence should be provided regarding proposal evaluations?

751. When and what information can be considered with offerors regarding past performance?

752. What are the steps in performing a cost/tech tradeoff?

753. Why promote competition?

754. Have all evaluators been trained?

755. Is a letter of commitment from each proposed team member and key subcontractor included?

756. Have team members been adequately trained?

757. Do you consider all weaknesses, significant weaknesses, and deficiencies?

758. How should the preproposal conference be conducted?

759. What can not be disclosed?

760. When is it appropriate to issue a Draft Request for

Proposal (DRFP)?

761. Do proposed hours support content and schedule?

762. Which contract type places the most risk on the seller?

763. Do you ensure you evaluate what you asked for, not what you want to see or expect to see?

764. Are they compliant with all technical requirements?

765. How do you manage procurement?

766. How can the methods of publicizing the buy be tailored to yield more effective price competition?

767. Can you prevent comparison of proposals?

768. In the technical/management area, what criteria do you use to determine the final evaluation ratings?

2.38 Stakeholder Management Plan: Azure Data Lake

769. Is the schedule updated on a periodic basis?

770. What methods are to be used for managing and monitoring subcontractors (eg agreements, contracts etc)?

771. What is the difference between product and Azure Data Lake project scope?

772. Is the quality assurance team identified?

773. Alignment to strategic goals & objectives?

774. Are mitigation strategies identified?

775. Why would you develop a Azure Data Lake project Business Plan?

776. What is meant by managing the triple constraint?

777. Are the appropriate IT resources adequate to meet planned commitments?

778. What potential impact does the Azure Data Lake project have on the stakeholder?

779. Is the process working, and are people executing in compliance of the process?

780. Does the Azure Data Lake project have a formal

Azure Data Lake project Plan?

781. Are there nonconformance issues?

782. Are multiple estimation methods being employed?

783. What are reporting requirements?

784. How will you engage this stakeholder and gain commitment?

785. Who is responsible for arranging and managing the review(s)?

786. How accurate and complete is the information?

787. Have you eliminated all duplicative tasks or manual efforts, where appropriate?

788. Are there unnecessary steps that are creating bottlenecks and/or causing people to wait?

2.39 Change Management Plan: Azure Data Lake

789. When developing your communication plan do you address : When should the given message be communicated?

790. Have the systems been configured and tested?

791. Which relationships will change?

792. What is the reason for the communication?

793. Why is the initiative is being undertaken - What are the business drivers?

794. Has the training provider been established?

795. How can you best frame the message so that it addresses the audiences interests?

796. How do you know the requirements you documented are the right ones?

797. Are there any restrictions on who can receive the communications?

798. Identify the current level of skills and knowledge and behaviours of the group that will be impacted on. What prerequisite knowledge do corresponding groups need?

799. Have the approved procedures and policies been

published?

800. What policies and procedures need to be changed?

801. What are the training strategies?

802. What is the negative impact of communicating too soon or too late?

803. What roles within your organization are affected, and how?

804. Where will the funds come from?

805. Will the readiness criteria be met prior to the training roll out?

806. How many people are required in each of the roles?

807. Why would a Azure Data Lake project run more smoothly when change management is emphasized from the beginning?

3.0 Executing Process Group: Azure Data Lake

808. How could stakeholders negatively impact your Azure Data Lake project?

809. Do Azure Data Lake project managers understand your organizational context for Azure Data Lake projects?

810. How do you enter durations, link tasks, and view critical path information?

811. Is the Azure Data Lake project making progress in helping to achieve the set results?

812. What are the main types of goods and services being outsourced?

813. Are escalated issues resolved promptly?

814. What does it mean to take a systems view of a Azure Data Lake project?

815. What are the main parts of the scope statement?

816. How is Azure Data Lake project performance information created and distributed?

817. When is the appropriate time to bring the scorecard to Board meetings?

818. What is involved in the solicitation process?

819. What type of information goes in the quality assurance plan?

820. How does the job market and current state of the economy affect human resource management?

821. How well defined and documented were the Azure Data Lake project management processes you chose to use?

822. Do schedule issues conflicts?

823. Why do you need a good WBS to use Azure Data Lake project management software?

824. Who will be the main sponsor?

825. What are the main types of contracts if you do decide to outsource?

826. What are crucial elements of successful Azure Data Lake project plan execution?

3.1 Team Member Status Report: Azure Data Lake

827. How it is to be done?

828. How will resource planning be done?

829. How much risk is involved?

830. How can you make it practical?

831. Why is it to be done?

832. How does this product, good, or service meet the needs of the Azure Data Lake project and your organization as a whole?

833. Are the attitudes of staff regarding Azure Data Lake project work improving?

834. Are your organizations Azure Data Lake projects more successful over time?

835. Are the products of your organizations Azure Data Lake projects meeting customers objectives?

836. Does your organization have the means (staff, money, contract, etc.) to produce or to acquire the product, good, or service?

837. What is to be done?

838. Will the staff do training or is that done by a third

party?

839. What specific interest groups do you have in place?

840. Does the product, good, or service already exist within your organization?

841. When a teams productivity and success depend on collaboration and the efficient flow of information, what generally fails them?

842. Does every department have to have a Azure Data Lake project Manager on staff?

843. Do you have an Enterprise Azure Data Lake project Management Office (EPMO)?

844. The problem with Reward & Recognition Programs is that the truly deserving people all too often get left out. How can you make it practical?

845. Is there evidence that staff is taking a more professional approach toward management of your organizations Azure Data Lake projects?

3.2 Change Request: Azure Data Lake

846. Who has responsibility for approving and ranking changes?

847. Customer acceptance plan how will the customer verify the change has been implemented successfully?

848. Have all related configuration items been properly updated?

849. Who is responsible for the implementation and monitoring of all measures?

850. Can static requirements change attributes like the size of the change be used to predict reliability in execution?

851. Where do changes come from?

852. Are there requirements attributes that can discriminate between high and low reliability?

853. Have scm procedures for noting the change, recording it, and reporting it been followed?

854. What is the function of the change control committee?

855. How does your organization control changes before and after software is released to a customer?

856. Who can suggest changes?

857. Describe how modifications, enhancements, defects and/or deficiencies shall be notified (e.g. Problem Reports, Change Requests etc) and managed. Detail warranty and/or maintenance periods?

858. How fast will change requests be approved?

859. What is the change request log?

860. How are changes requested (forms, method of communication)?

861. What is the relationship between requirements attributes and attributes like complexity and size?

862. Does the schedule include Azure Data Lake project management time and change request analysis time?

863. What is the purpose of change control?

864. What are the duties of the change control team?

865. How does a team identify the discrete elements of a configuration?

3.3 Change Log: Azure Data Lake

866. Do the described changes impact on the integrity or security of the system?

867. How does this change affect the timeline of the schedule?

868. Is the change request open, closed or pending?

869. Is the change backward compatible without limitations?

870. Should a more thorough impact analysis be conducted?

871. When was the request submitted?

872. When was the request approved?

873. Is the requested change request a result of changes in other Azure Data Lake project(s)?

874. Is this a mandatory replacement?

875. Is the submitted change a new change or a modification of a previously approved change?

876. How does this change affect scope?

877. Is the change request within Azure Data Lake project scope?

878. Who initiated the change request?

879. Does the suggested change request seem to represent a necessary enhancement to the product?

880. How does this relate to the standards developed for specific business processes?

881. Will the Azure Data Lake project fail if the change request is not executed?

3.4 Decision Log: Azure Data Lake

882. With whom was the decision shared or considered?

883. Adversarial environment. is your opponent open to a non-traditional workflow, or will it likely challenge anything you do?

884. Does anything need to be adjusted?

885. Who is the decisionmaker?

886. Is everything working as expected?

887. What is your overall strategy for quality control / quality assurance procedures?

888. How do you know when you are achieving it?

889. Do strategies and tactics aimed at less than full control reduce the costs of management or simply shift the cost burden?

890. Is your opponent open to a non-traditional workflow, or will it likely challenge anything you do?

891. Linked to original objective?

892. How effective is maintaining the log at facilitating organizational learning?

893. What makes you different or better than others companies selling the same thing?

894. It becomes critical to track and periodically revisit both operational effectiveness; Are you noticing all that you need to, and are you interpreting what you see effectively?

895. Decision-making process; how will the team make decisions?

896. What are the cost implications?

897. What alternatives/risks were considered?

898. Meeting purpose; why does this team meet?

899. At what point in time does loss become unacceptable?

900. How does the use a Decision Support System influence the strategies/tactics or costs?

901. What was the rationale for the decision?

3.5 Quality Audit: Azure Data Lake

902. What does an analysis of your organizations staff profile suggest in terms of its planning, and how is this being addressed?

903. Have personnel cleanliness and health requirements been established?

904. How does your organization know that its system for examining work done is appropriately effective and constructive?

905. Do prior clients have a positive opinion of your organization?

906. What mechanisms exist for identification of staff development needs?

907. How does your organization know that its Strategic Plan is providing the best guidance for the future of your organization?

908. How does your organization know that its management of its ethical responsibilities is appropriately effective and constructive?

909. How does your organization know that its system for governing staff behaviour is appropriately effective and constructive?

910. How does your organization know that its staff support services planning and management systems are appropriately effective and constructive?

911. Are storage areas and reconditioning operations designed to prevent mix-ups and assure orderly handling of both the distressed and reconditioned devices?

912. How does your organization know that its system for ensuring a positive organizational climate is appropriately effective and constructive?

913. Are all employees including salespersons made aware that they must report all complaints received from any source for inclusion in the complaint handling system?

914. Are there sufficient personnel having the necessary education, background, training, and experience to assure that all operations are correctly performed?

915. How does your organization know that its general support services planning and management systems are appropriately effective and constructive?

916. Do the suppliers use a formal quality system?

917. How does your organization know that its system for recruiting the best staff possible are appropriately effective and constructive?

918. How does your organization know that its processes for managing severance are appropriately effective, constructive and fair?

919. How does your organization know that its security arrangements are appropriately effective and

constructive?

920. What are you trying to accomplish with this audit?

921. How does your organization know that its system for supporting staff research capability is appropriately effective and constructive?

3.6 Team Directory: Azure Data Lake

922. Who will be the stakeholders on your next Azure Data Lake project?

923. When will you produce deliverables?

924. Contract requirements complied with?

925. Why is the work necessary?

926. Who are your stakeholders (customers, sponsors, end users, team members)?

927. Is construction on schedule?

928. Process decisions: are there any statutory or regulatory issues relevant to the timely execution of work?

929. Decisions: what could be done better to improve the quality of the constructed product?

930. Who will report Azure Data Lake project status to all stakeholders?

931. Process decisions: how well was task order work performed?

932. How do unidentified risks impact the outcome of the Azure Data Lake project?

933. What are you going to deliver or accomplish?

934. Who will talk to the customer?

935. Process decisions: do job conditions warrant additional actions to collect job information and document on-site activity?

936. Where should the information be distributed?

937. Process decisions: are all start-up, turn over and close out requirements of the contract satisfied?

938. Who is the Sponsor?

939. Who are the Team Members?

940. Decisions: is the most suitable form of contract being used?

941. Process decisions: do invoice amounts match accepted work in place?

3.7 Team Operating Agreement: Azure Data Lake

942. Did you determine the technology methods that best match the messages to be communicated?

943. Is compensation based on team and individual performance?

944. Confidentiality: how will confidential information be handled?

945. What are the safety issues/risks that need to be addressed and/or that the team needs to consider?

946. Do you prevent individuals from dominating the meeting?

947. Are there more than two national cultures represented by your team?

948. Did you delegate tasks such as taking meeting minutes, presenting a topic and soliciting input?

949. Did you draft the meeting agenda?

950. How will your group handle planned absences?

951. Must your team members rely on the expertise of other members to complete tasks?

952. Must your members collaborate successfully to complete Azure Data Lake projects?

953. How will group handle unplanned absences?

954. What individual strengths does each team member bring to the group?

955. Are leadership responsibilities shared among team members (versus a single leader)?

956. What are some potential sources of conflict among team members?

957. Do you record meetings for the already stated unable to attend?

958. What administrative supports will be put in place to support the team and the teams supervisor?

959. Do you ensure that all participants know how to use the required technology?

960. Do you ask participants to close laptops and place mobile devices on silent on the table while the meeting is in progress?

961. Resource allocation: how will individual team members account for time and expenses, and how will this be allocated in the team budget?

3.8 Team Performance Assessment: Azure Data Lake

962. Can team performance be reliably measured in simulator and live exercises using the same assessment tool?

963. To what degree do team members frequently explore the teams purpose and its implications?

964. To what degree do team members feel that the purpose of the team is important, if not exciting?

965. To what degree will the team ensure that all members equitably share the work essential to the success of the team?

966. What structural changes have you made or are you preparing to make?

967. If you have criticized someones work for method variance in your role as reviewer, what was the circumstance?

968. Do you give group members authority to make at least some important decisions?

969. Social categorization and intergroup behaviour: Does minimal intergroup discrimination make social identity more positive?

970. To what degree is there a sense that only the team can succeed?

971. To what degree can team members frequently and easily communicate with one another?

972. How hard do you try to make a good selection?

973. How do you manage human resources?

974. To what degree are the skill areas critical to team performance present?

975. To what degree are the teams goals and objectives clear, simple, and measurable?

976. To what degree can the team ensure that all members are individually and jointly accountable for the teams purpose, goals, approach, and work-products?

977. To what degree is the team cognizant of small wins to be celebrated along the way?

978. To what degree will the team adopt a concrete, clearly understood, and agreed-upon approach that will result in achievement of the teams goals?

979. Individual task proficiency and team process behavior: what is important for team functioning?

980. How do you keep key people outside the group informed about its accomplishments?

981. To what degree does the team possess adequate membership to achieve its ends?

3.9 Team Member Performance Assessment: Azure Data Lake

982. How often are assessments to be conducted?

983. For what period of time is a member rated?

984. Does the rater (supervisor) have to wait for the interim or final performance assessment review to tell an employee that the employees performance is unsatisfactory?

985. How do you work together to improve teaching and learning?

986. To what extent did the evaluation influence the instructional path, such as with adaptive testing?

987. How are assessments designed, delivered, and otherwise used to maximize training?

988. What specific plans do you have for developing effective cross-platform assessments in a blended learning environment?

989. Who is responsible?

990. Is it clear how goals will be accomplished?

991. How are evaluation results utilized?

992. How is the timing of assessments organized (e.g., pre/post-test, single point during training, multiple

reassessment during training)?

993. What are acceptable governance changes?

994. Which training platform formats (i.e., mobile, virtual, videogame-based) were implemented in your effort(s)?

995. What tools are available to determine whether all contract functional and compliance areas of performance objectives, measures, and incentives have been met?

996. What steps have you taken to improve performance?

997. What resources do you need?

998. To what degree are the goals realistic?

999. To what degree are sub-teams possible or necessary?

1000. To what degree does the teams approach to its work allow for modification and improvement over time?

3.10 Issue Log: Azure Data Lake

1001. Why multiple evaluators?

1002. Do you often overlook a key stakeholder or stakeholder group?

1003. Are the stakeholders getting the information they need, are they consulted, are concerns addressed?

1004. Which stakeholders can influence others?

1005. Who is the issue assigned to?

1006. What is a Stakeholder?

1007. What are the typical contents?

1008. Who do you turn to if you have questions?

1009. What is the impact on the risks?

1010. What are the stakeholders interrelationships?

1011. Who were proponents/opponents?

1012. Are you constantly rushing from meeting to meeting?

1013. How much time does it take to do it?

1014. Are the Azure Data Lake project issues uniquely identified, including to which product they refer?

1015. What help do you and your team need from the stakeholders?

1016. Who have you worked with in past, similar initiatives?

4.0 Monitoring and Controlling Process Group: Azure Data Lake

1017. In what way has the program come up with innovative measures for problem-solving?

1018. Accuracy: what design will lead to accurate information?

1019. Have operating capacities been created and/or reinforced in partners?

1020. Did you implement the program as designed?

1021. User: who wants the information and what are they interested in?

1022. Key stakeholders to work with. How many potential communications channels exist on the Azure Data Lake project?

1023. What were things that you did very well and want to do the same again on the next Azure Data Lake project?

1024. How is agile program management done?

1025. How can you make your needs known?

1026. How well did the team follow the chosen processes?

1027. Is there undesirable impact on staff or

resources?

1028. How were collaborations developed, and how are they sustained?

1029. What good practices or successful experiences or transferable examples have been identified?

1030. What are the goals of the program?

4.1 Project Performance Report: Azure Data Lake

1031. To what degree are the demands of the task compatible with and converge with the mission and functions of the formal organization?

1032. To what degree does the teams work approach provide opportunity for members to engage in results-based evaluation?

1033. To what degree is the information network consistent with the structure of the formal organization?

1034. What degree are the relative importance and priority of the goals clear to all team members?

1035. What is the degree to which rules govern information exchange between individuals within your organization?

1036. To what degree can the cognitive capacity of individuals accommodate the flow of information?

1037. To what degree does the teams purpose constitute a broader, deeper aspiration than just accomplishing short-term goals?

1038. To what degree do team members agree with the goals, relative importance, and the ways in which achievement will be measured?

1039. To what degree can team members meet frequently enough to accomplish the teams ends?

1040. To what degree will the approach capitalize on and enhance the skills of all team members in a manner that takes into consideration other demands on members of the team?

1041. To what degree does the information network provide individuals with the information they require?

1042. To what degree do team members understand one anothers roles and skills?

1043. To what degree does the informal organization make use of individual resources and meet individual needs?

1044. What is the degree to which rules govern information exchange between groups?

4.2 Variance Analysis: Azure Data Lake

1045. How does the use of a single conversion element (rather than the traditional labor and overhead elements) affect standard costing?

1046. Are records maintained to show how undistributed budgets are controlled?

1047. Who is generally responsible for monitoring and taking action on variances?

1048. Are the overhead pools formally and adequately identified?

1049. Does the scheduling system identify in a timely manner the status of work?

1050. Is work properly classified as measured effort, LOE, or apportioned effort and appropriately separated?

1051. What types of services and expense are shared between business segments?

1052. Are your organizations and items of cost assigned to each pool identified?

1053. Historical experience?

1054. When, during the last four quarters, did a primary business event occur causing a fluctuation?

1055. Are estimates of costs at completion generated in a rational, consistent manner?

1056. Are the bases and rates for allocating costs from each indirect pool consistently applied?

1057. Does the contractor use objective results, design reviews and tests to trace schedule performance?

1058. Are indirect costs charged to the appropriate indirect pools and incurring organization?

1059. Did an existing competitor change strategy?

1060. Are management actions taken to reduce indirect costs when there are significant adverse variances?

1061. How does your organization measure performance?

1062. Are all elements of indirect expense identified to overhead cost budgets of Azure Data Lake projections?

1063. How do you haverify authorization to proceed with all authorized work?

1064. Is work progressively subdivided into detailed work packages as requirements are defined?

4.3 Earned Value Status: Azure Data Lake

1065. If earned value management (EVM) is so good in determining the true status of a Azure Data Lake project and Azure Data Lake project its completion, why is it that hardly any one uses it in information systems related Azure Data Lake projects?

1066. Are you hitting your Azure Data Lake projects targets?

1067. Validation is a process of ensuring that the developed system will actually achieve the stakeholders desired outcomes; Are you building the right product? What do you validate?

1068. Where are your problem areas?

1069. What is the unit of forecast value?

1070. Earned value can be used in almost any Azure Data Lake project situation and in almost any Azure Data Lake project environment. it may be used on large Azure Data Lake projects, medium sized Azure Data Lake projects, tiny Azure Data Lake projects (in cut-down form), complex and simple Azure Data Lake projects and in any market sector. some people, of course, know all about earned value, they have used it for years - but perhaps not as effectively as they could have?

1071. How much is it going to cost by the finish?

1072. Where is evidence-based earned value in your organization reported?

1073. Verification is a process of ensuring that the developed system satisfies the stakeholders agreements and specifications; Are you building the product right? What do you haverify?

1074. How does this compare with other Azure Data Lake projects?

1075. When is it going to finish?

4.4 Risk Audit: Azure Data Lake

1076. Have you considered the health and safety of everyone in your organization and do you meet work health and safety regulations?

1077. What is the effect of globalisation; is business becoming too complex and can the auditor rely on auditing standards?

1078. Are formal technical reviews part of this process?

1079. What does monitoring consist of?

1080. How effective are your risk controls?

1081. What resources are needed to achieve program results?

1082. What are risks and how do you manage them?

1083. Are you willing to seek legal advice when required?

1084. Do you have a clear plan for the future that describes what you want to do and how you are going to do it?

1085. Does your organization have a register of insurance policies detailing all current insurance policies?

1086. Is all required equipment available?

1087. Does your organization meet the terms of any contracts with which it is involved?

1088. Estimated size of product in number of programs, files, transactions?

1089. What can be measured?

1090. Are all programs planned and conducted according to recognized safety standards?

1091. Have staff received necessary training?

1092. What are the benefits of a Enterprise wide approach to Risk Management?

1093. Are procedures in place to ensure the security of staff and information and compliance with privacy legislation if applicable?

4.5 Contractor Status Report: Azure Data Lake

1094. How does the proposed individual meet each requirement?

1095. What process manages the contracts?

1096. Are there contractual transfer concerns?

1097. How long have you been using the services?

1098. What is the average response time for answering a support call?

1099. What was the overall budget or estimated cost?

1100. What was the budget or estimated cost for your organizations services?

1101. How is risk transferred?

1102. If applicable; describe your standard schedule for new software version releases. Are new software version releases included in the standard maintenance plan?

1103. Who can list a Azure Data Lake project as organization experience, your organization or a previous employee of your organization?

1104. What are the minimum and optimal bandwidth requirements for the proposed soluiton?

1105. Describe how often regular updates are made to the proposed solution. Are corresponding regular updates included in the standard maintenance plan?

1106. What was the final actual cost?

1107. What was the actual budget or estimated cost for your organizations services?

4.6 Formal Acceptance: Azure Data Lake

1108. What features, practices, and processes proved to be strengths or weaknesses?

1109. What was done right?

1110. How does your team plan to obtain formal acceptance on your Azure Data Lake project?

1111. Do you perform formal acceptance or burn-in tests?

1112. What function(s) does it fill or meet?

1113. Does it do what Azure Data Lake project team said it would?

1114. Was the sponsor/customer satisfied?

1115. Was the Azure Data Lake project managed well?

1116. Was business value realized?

1117. Who supplies data?

1118. What is the Acceptance Management Process?

1119. What can you do better next time?

1120. Was the Azure Data Lake project goal achieved?

1121. Do you buy pre-configured systems or build your own configuration?

1122. Have all comments been addressed?

1123. Is formal acceptance of the Azure Data Lake project product documented and distributed?

1124. Do you buy-in installation services?

1125. Was the Azure Data Lake project work done on time, within budget, and according to specification?

1126. How well did the team follow the methodology?

1127. Did the Azure Data Lake project manager and team act in a professional and ethical manner?

5.0 Closing Process Group: Azure Data Lake

1128. Was the schedule met?

1129. What were things that you did well, and could improve, and how?

1130. What is the amount of funding and what Azure Data Lake project phases are funded?

1131. How well defined and documented were the Azure Data Lake project management processes you chose to use?

1132. Were escalated issues resolved promptly?

1133. Did the Azure Data Lake project team have enough people to execute the Azure Data Lake project plan?

1134. How critical is the Azure Data Lake project success to the success of your organization?

1135. How well did the chosen processes fit the needs of the Azure Data Lake project?

1136. Did you do what you said you were going to do?

1137. What is the risk of failure to your organization?

1138. What were the desired outcomes?

1139. What could have been improved?

1140. What is the Azure Data Lake project Management Process?

1141. Mitigate. what will you do to minimize the impact should a risk event occur?

1142. Did the Azure Data Lake project team have the right skills?

1143. What was learned?

1144. Did the delivered product meet the specified requirements and goals of the Azure Data Lake project?

1145. What is the overall risk of the Azure Data Lake project to your organization?

5.1 Procurement Audit: Azure Data Lake

1146. Audits: when was your last independent public accountant (ipa) audit and what were the results?

1147. Are there procedures for trade-in arrangements?

1148. Is a physical inventory taken periodically to verify fixed asset records?

1149. Has your organization examined in detail the definition of performance?

1150. Was invitation to tender to each specific contract issued after the evaluation of the indicative tenders was completed?

1151. Are all checks stored in a secure area?

1152. Are procurement policies and practices in line with (international) good practice standards?

1153. Has the department identified and described the different elements in the procurement process?

1154. In case of time and material and labour hour contracts, does surveillance give an adequate and reasonable assurance that the contractor is using efficient methods and effective cost controls?

1155. When negotiation took place in successive

stages, was this practice stated in the procurement documents and was it done in accordance with the award criteria stated?

1156. Are vendor price lists regularly updated?

1157. Is confidentiality guaranteed during the whole process?

1158. Does the strategy ensure that the concepts of standardisation and coordination of procurement are used to take advantage of the departments collective buying power?

1159. Is the efficiency of the procurement process regularly evaluated?

1160. Is the routing of copies of purchase order forms defined?

1161. Do the buyers always select or authorize the source of supply on other than contract purchases?

1162. Are buyers prohibited from accepting gifts from vendors?

1163. Do appropriate controls ensure that procurement decisions are not biased by conflicts of interest or corruption?

1164. Which are necessary components of a financial audit report under the Single Audit Act?

1165. Was the estimated contract value based on realistic and updated prices?

5.2 Contract Close-Out: Azure Data Lake

1166. How/when used ?

1167. Have all contracts been closed?

1168. Have all contract records been included in the Azure Data Lake project archives?

1169. How is the contracting office notified of the automatic contract close-out?

1170. Why Outsource?

1171. What happens to the recipient of services?

1172. Was the contract type appropriate?

1173. Are the signers the authorized officials?

1174. Parties: who is involved?

1175. Was the contract complete without requiring numerous changes and revisions?

1176. What is capture management?

1177. Was the contract sufficiently clear so as not to result in numerous disputes and misunderstandings?

1178. Change in circumstances?

1179. Change in attitude or behavior?

1180. Have all contracts been completed?

1181. Change in knowledge?

1182. How does it work?

1183. Have all acceptance criteria been met prior to final payment to contractors?

1184. Parties: Authorized?

1185. Has each contract been audited to verify acceptance and delivery?

5.3 Project or Phase Close-Out: Azure Data Lake

1186. How much influence did the stakeholder have over others?

1187. What is a Risk Management Process?

1188. What benefits or impacts does the stakeholder group expect to obtain as a result of the Azure Data Lake project?

1189. What is a Risk?

1190. What process was planned for managing issues/risks?

1191. Which changes might a stakeholder be required to make as a result of the Azure Data Lake project?

1192. Planned completion date?

1193. Planned remaining costs?

1194. What went well?

1195. Did the delivered product meet the specified requirements and goals of the Azure Data Lake project?

1196. Have business partners been involved extensively, and what data was required for them?

1197. What are the mandatory communication needs for each stakeholder?

1198. What is the information level of detail required for each stakeholder?

1199. What can you do better next time, and what specific actions can you take to improve?

1200. What information is each stakeholder group interested in?

1201. Who controlled key decisions that were made?

1202. Does the lesson describe a function that would be done differently the next time?

5.4 Lessons Learned: Azure Data Lake

1203. If you had to do this Azure Data Lake project again, what is the one thing that you would change (related to process, not to technical solutions)?

1204. How effective was the support you received during implementation of the product/service?

1205. What Azure Data Lake project circumstances were not anticipated?

1206. How was the quality of products/processes assured?

1207. What should have been accomplished during predeployment that was not accomplished?

1208. Why does your organization need a lessons learned (LL) capability?

1209. Was sufficient time allocated to review Azure Data Lake project deliverables?

1210. If issue escalation was required, how effectively were issues resolved?

1211. Overall, how effective were the efforts to prepare you and your organization for the impact of the product/service of the Azure Data Lake project?

1212. How well did the Azure Data Lake project Manager respond to questions or comments related to the Azure Data Lake project?

1213. Was there a Azure Data Lake project Definition document. Was there a Azure Data Lake project Plan. Were they used during the Azure Data Lake project?

1214. How effective was each Azure Data Lake project Team member in fulfilling his/her role?

1215. What is the proportion of in-house and contractor personnel authorized for the Azure Data Lake project?

1216. How efficient and effective were Azure Data Lake project team meetings?

1217. How useful was the format and content of the Azure Data Lake project Status Report to you?

1218. How clear were you on your role in the Azure Data Lake project?

1219. How closely did deliverables match what was defined within the Azure Data Lake project Scope?

1220. How efficient were Azure Data Lake project team meetings conducted?

1221. How did the estimated Azure Data Lake project Budget compare with the total actual expenditures?

Index

319

322